CONTEMPORARY'S

Achieving

MCAS

Success in

MATHEMATICS

HOWARD I. BERRENT, Ph.D.

Mc Graw Hill **Wright Group**

The McGraw·Hill Companies

Editor: Rebecca Grober

Executive Editor: Linda Kwil

Production Coordinator: Linda Chandler

Marketing Manager: Sheila Caswell

Cover Design: Tracey Harris-Sainz

Interior Design: Think Design Group LLC

Wright Group

ISBN: 0-07-704412-6

Send all inquiries to:
McGraw-Hill/Wright Group
130 East Randolph Street, Suite 400
Chicago, IL 60601

Printed in the United States of America

1 2 3 4 5 6 7 8 9 10 POH 08 07 06 05

The **McGraw·Hill** Companies

Table of Contents

To the Student

Introduction to the Grade 10 MCAS in Mathematics

The MCAS in Mathematics tests the following five major content stands from the Mathematics Curriculum Framework of the State of Massachusetts:

- Number Sense and Operations
- Patterns, Relations, and Algebra
- Geometry
- Measurement
- Data Analysis, Statistics, and Probability

Test Sessions and Types of Questions

The MCAS Mathematics Test is given in two separate sessions, which are administered on consecutive days. Each session includes multiple-choice and open-response questions. Session 1 also includes short-answer questions.

Session 1 has a total of 21 questions. There are 14 multiple-choice, 3 open-response, and 4 short-answer questions. Session 2 has 16 multiple-choice and 3 open-response questions. The multiple-choice questions require you to choose a correct answer from four options. Short-answer questions require that you write a brief response to the question. Open-ended questions require you to answer several parts of the question and to show your work. Your answer will be graded using a rubric that is designed for each open-ended question.

Reference Materials

Each student is provided with a *Grade 10 Mathematics Reference Sheet*. A copy of this reference sheet can be found on pages 2 and 130 of this book.

Calculators are not allowed during Session 1. During Session 2, students are permitted to use calculators with at least four functions and a square root key.

Standards Tested on the Grade 10 MCAS in Mathematics

The Mathematics Curriculum Framework of the State of Massachusetts lists general expectations for student achievement within specific areas. There are 30 standards tested on the Grade 10 MCAS in Mathematics:

Number Sense and Operations

- **Understand numbers, ways of representing numbers, relationships among numbers, and number systems**

- **Understand meanings of operations and how they relate to one another**

- **Compute fluently and make reasonable estimates**

Students engage in problem solving, communicating, reasoning, connecting, and representing as they:

10.N.1   Identify and use the properties of operations on real numbers, including the associative, commutative, and distributive properties; the existence of the identity and inverse elements for addition and multiplication; the existence of *n*th roots of positive real numbers for any positive integer *n*; and the inverse relationship between taking the *n*th root of the *n*th power of a positive real number.

10.N.2   Simplify numerical expressions, including those involving positive integer exponents or the absolute value, e.g., $3(2^4 - 1) = 45$, $4|3 - 5| + 6 = 14$; apply such simplifications in the solution of problems.

10.N.3   Find the approximate value for solutions to problems involving square roots and cube roots without the use of a calculator, e.g., $\sqrt{3^2} - 1 \approx 2.8$.

10.N.4   Use estimation to judge the reasonableness of results of computations and of solutions to problems involving real numbers.

Patterns, Relations, and Algebra

- **Understand patterns, relations, and functions**

- **Represent and analyze mathematical situations and structures using algebraic symbols**

- **Use mathematical models to represent and understand quantitative relalntionships**

- **Analyze change in various contexts**

Students engage in problem solving, communicating, reasoning, connecting, and representing as they:

10.P.1   Describe, complete, extend, analyze, generalize, and create a wide variety of patterns, including iterative, recursive (e.g., Fibonacci Numbers), linear, quadratic, and exponential functional relationships.

10.P.2   Demonstrate an understanding of the relationship between various representations of a line. Determine a line's slope and *x*- and *y*-intercepts from its graph or from a linear equation that represents the line. Find a linear equation describing a line from a graph or a geometric description of the line, e.g., by using the "point-slope" or "slope *y*-intercept" formulas. Explain the significance of a positive, negative, zero, or undefined slope.

10.P.3   Add, subtract, and multiply polynomials. Divide polynomials by monomials.

10.P.4   Demonstrate facility in symbolic manipulation of polynomial and rational expressions by rearranging and collecting terms; factoring (e.g., $a^2 - b^2 = (a + b)(a - b)$, $x^2 + 10x + 21 = (x + 3)(x + 7)$, $5x^4 + 10x^3 - 5x^2 = 5x^2 (x^2 + 2x - 1)$); identifying and canceling common factors in rational expressions; and applying the properties of positive integer exponents.

10.P.5 Find solutions to quadratic equations (with real roots) by factoring, completing the square, or using the quadratic formula. Demonstrate an understanding of the equivalence of the methods.

10.P.6 Solve equations and inequalities including those involving absolute value of linear expressions (e.g., $|x - 2| > 5$) and apply to the solution of problems.

10.P.7 Solve everyday problems that can be modeled using linear, reciprocal, quadratic, or exponential functions. Apply appropriate tabular, graphical, or symbolic methods to the solution. Include compound interest, and direct and inverse variation problems. Use technology when appropriate.

10.P.8 Solve everyday problems that can be modeled using systems of linear equations or inequalities. Apply algebraic and graphical methods to the solution. Use technology when appropriate. Include mixture, rate, and work problems.

Geometry

- **Analyze characteristics and properties of two- and three-dimensional geometric shapes and develop mathematical arguments about geometric relationships**

- **Specify locations and describe spatial relationships using coordinate geometry and other representational systems**

- **Apply transformations and use symmetry to analyze mathematical situations**

- **Use visualization, spatial reasoning, and geometric modeling to solve problems**

Students engage in problem solving, communicating, reasoning, connecting, and representing as they:

10.G.1 Identify figures using properties of sides, angles, and diagonals. Identify the figures' type(s) of symmetry.

10.G.2 Draw congruent and similar figures using a compass, straightedge, protractor, and other tools such as computer software. Make conjectures about methods of construction. Justify the conjectures by logical arguments.

10.G.3 Recognize and solve problems involving angles formed by transversals of coplanar lines. Identify and determine the measure of central and inscribed angles and their associated minor and major arcs. Recognize and solve problems associated with radii, chords, and arcs within or on the same circle.

10.G.4 Apply congruence and similarity correspondences (e.g., $\triangle ABC \approx \triangle XYZ$) and properties of the figures to find missing parts of geometric figures and provide logical justification.

10.G.5 Solve simple triangle problems using the triangle angle sum property and/or the Pythagorean theorem.

10.G.6 Use the properties of special triangles (e.g., isosceles, equilateral, $30°-60°-90°$, $45°-45°-90°$) to solve problems.

10.G.7 Using rectangular coordinates, calculate midpoints of segments, slopes of lines and segments, and distances between two points, and apply the results to the solutions of problems.

10.G.8 Find linear equations that represent lines either perpendicular or parallel to a given line and through a point, e.g., by using the "point-slope" form of the equation.

10.G.9 Draw the results and interpret transformations on figures in the coordinate plane, e.g., translations, reflections, rotations, scale factors, and the results of successive transformations. Apply transformations to the solutions of problems.

10.G.10 Demonstrate the ability to visualize solid objects and recognize their projections and cross sections.

10.G.11 Use vertex-edge graphs to model and solve problems.

Measurement

- **Understand measurable attributes of objects and the units, systems, and processes of measurement**

- **Apply appropriate techniques, tools, and formulas to determine measurements**

Students engage in problem solving, communicating, reasoning, connecting, and representing as they:

10.M.1 Calculate perimeter, circumference, and area of common geometric figures such as parallelograms, trapezoids, circles, and triangles.

10.M.2 Given the formula, find the lateral area, surface area, and volume of prisms, pyramids, spheres, cylinders, and cones, e.g., find the volume of a sphere with a specified surface area.

10.M.3 Relate changes in the measurement of one attribute of an object to changes in other attributes, e.g., how changing the radius or height of a cylinder affects its surface area or volume.

10.M.4 Describe the effects of approximate error in measurement and rounding on measurements and on computed values from measurements.

Data Analysis, Statistics, and Probability

- **Formulate questions that can be addressed with data and collect, organize, and display relevant data to answer them**

- **Select and use appropriate statistical methods to analyze data**

- **Develop and evaluate inferences and predictions that are based on data**

- **Understand and apply basic concepts of probabilty**

Students engage in problem solving, communicating, reasoning, connecting and representing as they:

10.D.1 Select, create, and interpret an appropriate graphical representation (e.g., scatterplot, table, stem-and-leaf plots, box-and-whisker plots, circle graph, line graph, and line plot) for a set of data and use appropriate statistics (e.g., mean, median, range, and mode) to communicate information about the data. Use these notions to compare different sets of data.

10.D.2 Approximate a line of best fit (trend line) given a set of data (e.g. scatterplot). Use technology when appropriate.

10.D.3 Describe and explain how the relative sizes of a sample and the population affect the validity of predictions from a set of data.

How to Use This Book

The Diagnostic Pretest

This book contains a pretest, lessons based on the Massachusetts Mathematical standards, and a posttest. The first thing you should do is take the pretest. Remove the Pretest Answer Booklet (pages 153–159) out of the back of your book and use it to record all of your answers. Allow yourself two days to take the test. On the first day, you will take Session 1 Pretest and on the second day you will take Session 2 Pretest. You may use a calculator in Session 2. Give your teacher your Pretest Answer Booklet to be scored. Your teacher can tell you what standards you have mastered and which ones you should continue to work on.

Lesson and Reviews

Each lesson covers one of the 30 standards that appear on the MCAS in Mathematics. Before the lesson begins, the standard is stated and explained.

Each lesson is divided into three steps:

Step One: Sample Problem
One to three sample problems are presented. For the sample problems, explanations are given for each answer choice.

Step Two: Sidebar Instruction
Work problems and answer questions with the help of hints, called sidebars, in the margins.

Step Three: On Your Own
Practice working problems and answering questions on your own.

Review

At the end of every two to three lessons is a review. The review contains approximately ten questions based on the standards taught in the previous lessons.

The Diagnostic Posttest

After you have completed all of the lessons and reviews, remove the Posttest Answer Book (pages 161–168) from the back of your book and take the posttest. After your teacher has scored the posttest, he or she can tell you if there are standards you need to review. Go back and re-work the lessons related to those standards.

Pretest

MASSACHUSETTS COMPREHENSIVE ASSESSMENT SYSTEM
Grade 10 Mathematics Reference Sheet

AREA FORMULAS

triangle .... $A = \frac{1}{2}bh$

rectangle ...... $A = bh$

square .... $A = s^2$

trapezoid ..... $A = \frac{1}{2}h(b_1 + b_2)$

CIRCLE FORMULAS

$C = 2\pi r$

$A = \pi r^2$

VOLUME FORMULAS

cube .... $V = s^3$
(s = length of an edge)

rectangular prism .... $V = lwh$
$$OR$$
$$V = Bh$$
(B = area of the base)

sphere .... $V = \frac{4}{3}\pi r^3$

right circular cylinder .... $V = \pi r^2 h$

right circular cone .... $V = \frac{1}{3}\pi r^2 h$

right square pyramid .... $V = \frac{1}{3}s^2 h$

LATERAL SURFACE AREA FORMULAS

rectangular prism .... $LA = 2(hw) + 2(lh)$

right circular cylinder .... $LA = 2\pi rh$

right circular cone .... $LA = \pi r \ell$

right square pyramid .... $LA = 2s\ell$

(ℓ = slant height)

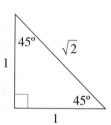

TOTAL SURFACE AREA FORMULAS

cube .... $SA = 6s^2$

rectangular prism .... $SA = 2(lw) + 2(hw) + 2(lh)$

sphere .... $SA = 4\pi r^2$

right circular cylinder .... $SA = 2\pi r^2 + 2\pi rh$

right circular cone .... $SA = \pi r^2 + \pi r \ell$

right square pyramid .... $SA = s^2 + 2s\ell$

(ℓ = slant height)

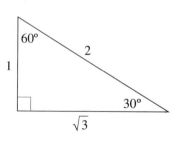

2

SESSION 1

You may use your reference sheet during this session.
*You may **not** use a calculator during this session.*

DIRECTIONS

This session contains fourteen multiple-choice questions, four short-answer questions, and three open-response questions. Mark your answers to these questions in the spaces provided in your Pretest Answer Booklet (page 153).

1 Which of the following is equal to $\sqrt{(169^2)^0} - 1$?

 A. 169

 B. 12

 C. 0

 D. -1

2 How many real numbers are there between 3.14 and 3.15?

 A. 10

 B. more than 10

 C. less than 10

 D. 1

Go On

3 George has four rabbit farms. The table below shows the populations of the farms over 3 weeks. Which of the four rabbit farms will have the largest population after 8 weeks?

	Farm 1	**Farm 2**	**Farm 3**	**Farm 4**
Start	10	10	10	10
Week 1	35	30	110	40
Week 2	60	90	210	70
Week 3	85	270	310	100

A. Rabbit farm 1

B. Rabbit farm 2

C. Rabbit farm 3

D. Rabbit farm 4

4 Which expression below is equivalent to $(2x + 2y)(2x - 2y)$?

A. $4x^2 + 8xy + 4y^2$

B. $4(x + xy + y)$

C. $4x + 4y$

D. $4x^2 - 4y^2$

5 At a local bank, Fred cashed an $800 check and received $10 and $20 bills in return. In all, he received 50 bills. Which pair of equations can be used to determine the number of each bill Fred received?

A. $x + y = 800$
   $10 + 20 = 50$

B. $x + y = 50$
   $10x + 20y = 800$

C. $x + y = 800$
   $10x + 20y = 50$

D. $x + y = 50$
   $50 + 800 = 10x + 20y$

6 Which of the following pairs of points identifies a line with slope $\frac{2}{3}$?

A. $(1, 4)$ and $(3, 7)$

B. $(-1, 5)$ and $(1, 2)$

C. $(-2, 6)$ and $(7, 12)$

D. $(2, 6)$ and $(5, 4)$

7 Two number cubes are rolled. What is the probability that the sum of the two numbers rolled is 8?

A. $\dfrac{1}{36}$

B. $\dfrac{2}{36}$

C. $\dfrac{6}{36}$

D. $\dfrac{5}{36}$

8 The length of each side of a cube is increased by a factor of 5. What is the change in the volume of the cube?

A. The volume is increased by a factor of 5.

B. The volume is increased by a factor of 10.

C. The volume is increased by a factor of 25.

D. The volume is increased by a factor of 125.

Go On

9 Plot the following points on the grid provided. Draw a single straight line that best represents the following data: (1, 4), (2, 1), (3, 7), (4, 9), (5, 15), (6, 16).

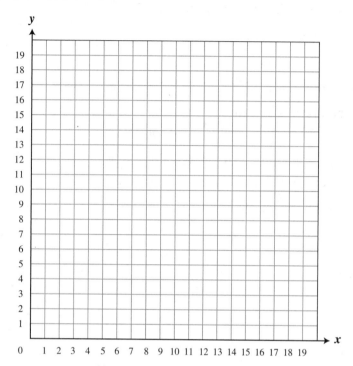

Which of the following lines could be the line of best fit for the data points above?

A. $y = -3x$

B. $y = -\dfrac{1}{3}x + 3$

C. $y = \dfrac{1}{3}x$

D. $y = 3x$

10 The hands of a clock indicate that the time is 2:30. What is the measure of the central angle formed by the hands of the clock?

A. 180 degrees

B. 125 degrees

C. 105 degrees

D. 90 degrees

11 Barney wants to store a crane in a building with an opening that forms an equilateral triangle. Each side of the triangle is 60 feet long. What is the approximate height of the peak of the opening? Will Barney be able to fit the crane through the opening of the building if the crane is 53 feet tall?

A. The height is about 60 feet, so the crane will fit.

B. The height is about 45 feet, so the crane won't fit.

C. The height is about 55 feet, so the crane will fit.

D. The height is about 52 feet, so the crane won't fit.

12 Calculate the slope of the line that passes through the points $(-4, 1)$ and $(1, -1)$.

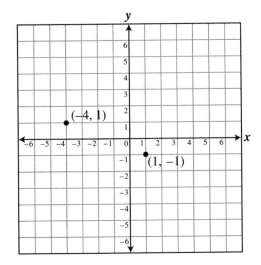

A. slope $= \dfrac{5}{2}$

B. slope $= \dfrac{2}{5}$

C. slope $= -\dfrac{2}{5}$

D. slope $= -\dfrac{5}{2}$

Go
On

13 Determine an equation of a line that is perpendicular to the graph of the line $y = 3x + 2$ and passes through the point $(-1, -1)$.

A. $y = -3x - 2$

B. $y = \dfrac{1}{3}x + 3$

C. $y = 2x + 3$

D. $y = -\dfrac{1}{3}x - \dfrac{3}{2}$

14 The perimeter of a rectangular garden is 128 feet. The width of the garden is 24 feet. What is the perimeter of a similar garden with a length of 20 feet?

A. 104 feet

B. 90 feet

C. 80 feet

D. 64 feet

Questions 15 and 16 are short-answer questions. Write your answers to these questions in the boxes provided in your Pretest Answer Booklet.

15 What is the value of the expression below?

$$4^3 - 2(5^2 - 2^4) + 7$$

16 Determine the equation of a line passing through the points (1, 6) and (2, 2).

Go On

Question 17 is an open-response question.

- **BE SURE TO ANSWER AND LABEL ALL PARTS OF EACH QUESTION.**
- Show all your work (diagrams, tables, or computations) in your Pretest Answer Booklet.
- If you do the work in your head, explain in writing how you did the work.

Write your answer to question 17 in the space provided in your Pretest Answer Booklet.

17 Fill in the missing steps below.

Given: $\angle F \cong \angle J$; $\overline{GI}$ bisects $\overline{FJ}$

Prove: $\triangle FHG \cong \triangle JHI$

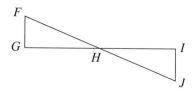

Statements	Reason
1. $\angle F \cong \angle J$	1. Given
2. $\overline{GI}$ bisects $\overline{FJ}$	2. Given
3. $\overline{FH} \approx \overline{JH}$	3.
4. $\angle FHG \approx \angle JHI$	4.
5. $\triangle FHG \approx \triangle JHI$	5.

Questions 18 and 19 are short-answer questions. Write your answers to these questions in the boxes provided in your Pretest Answer Booklet.

18 What is the value of the expression below?

$$\frac{3k}{k-7} + \frac{21}{(7-k)}$$

19 What is the value of the expression below?

$$5^3 - 4^3 - 3^2 - 2|1 - 11| - 10$$

Go
On

Questions 20 and 21 are open-response questions.

- **BE SURE TO ANSWER AND LABEL ALL PARTS OF EACH QUESTION.**
- **Show all your work (diagrams, tables, or computations) in your Pretest Answer Booklet.**
- **If you do the work in your head, explain in writing how you did the work.**

Write your answer to question 20 in the space provided in your Pretest Answer Booklet.

 In a standard deck of playing cards, there are 4 of each card numbered 2 through 10, 4 kings, 4 queens, 4 jacks and 4 aces for a total of 52 cards.

a. If you pick 2 cards in succession, replacing the first card before picking the second card, what is the probability of picking 2 aces?

b. If you pick 3 cards in succession WITHOUT replacing the previously selected cards, what is the probability of picking an ace, then a card numbered 7, then a card numbered 2?

c. If you pick 2 cards in a row, WITHOUT replacing the first card before picking the second card, what is the probability that the sum of the numbers of the cards selected equals 7? The jack is considered to have a value of 1.

Write your answer to question 21 in the space provided in your Pretest Answer Booklet.

21 An upscale swimsuit retailer has a store in Boston (B) and another one in Cambridge (C). The store sells both men's and women's swimsuits. The inventory data at the beginning of the month for each of the stores is contained in box I, and the value of each swimsuit is found in box V.

$$I = \begin{bmatrix} B & C \\ 200 & 110 \\ 150 & 80 \end{bmatrix} \begin{matrix} \\ \text{Women's} \\ \text{Men's} \end{matrix} \qquad V = \begin{bmatrix} \text{Women's} & \text{Men's} \\ \$150 & \$75 \end{bmatrix}$$

a. Using the information in boxes I and V, determine the total retail value of the swimsuits at the Cambridge store.

b. Determine the total value of the swimsuits at the Boston store.

c. Swimsuit sales for one month at each store are shown in box S below.

$$S = \begin{bmatrix} B & C \\ 150 & 60 \\ 100 & 75 \end{bmatrix} \begin{matrix} \\ \text{Women's} \\ \text{Men's} \end{matrix}$$

Write and solve an expression to determine the total retail value of the swimsuits at the end of the month for the store in Boston.

STOP

SESSION 2

You may use your reference sheet during this session.
You may use a calculator during this session.

DIRECTIONS:
This session contains eighteen multiple-choice questions and three open-response questions. Mark your answers to these questions in the spaces provided in your Pretest Answer Booklet.

22 If the figure below is translated 4 units to the left, then reflected across the *x*-axis, what will be the coordinates of point B^1?

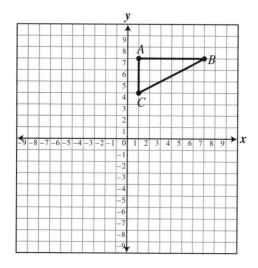

A. (11, 7)

B. (3, −7)

C. (−7, 3)

D. (−5, 7)

23 A rectangular garage is to be built whose area is expressed by function $f(x) = x^2 + 5x + 6$. Which pair of equations below can represent the length *l* and width *w* of the garage?

A. $l = x + 6, w = x + 5$

B. $l = x + 5, w = x + 6$

C. $l = x - 2, w = x - 3$

D. $l = x + 3, w = x + 2$

24 A manufacturer produces cement pipe used to feed a city's water supply. The ideal diameter of the pipe is 1 meter, but actual pipe may differ by 0.005 meter from this ideal and still be acceptable. Which of the following inequality could be used to represent this situation?

A. $|x + 1| \leq 0.005$

B. $|x - 1| \leq 0.005$

C. $|1 + 0.005| \leq x$

D. $|x - 0.005| \leq 1$

25 Which number is closest to the value of the expression shown below?

$$\sqrt{3^3 - 1^8 - 3(5) - 2^3}$$

A. 2.1

B. 1.9

C. 1.7

D. 1.5

26 An underground bunker in the shape of a rectangular prism has a width of 633 feet, a height of 481 feet, and a depth of 519 feet. Which of the following is the best estimate of the volume of the bunker?

A. 160,000,000 cubic feet

B. 180,000,000 cubic feet

C. 175,000,000 cubic feet

D. 100,000,000 cubic feet

27 The height of a triangle is given by the expression $5x^3y^6$, and the base is given by the expression $30x^4y$. Which expression can be used to find the area of the triangle?

A. $75x^{12}y^6$

B. $150x^7y^7$

C. $150x^{12}y^6$

D. $75x^7y^7$

Go On

28 A circular garden is to be constructed inside of a square yard whose area is 196 square feet. What is the area of the largest garden that can be built within this yard?

A. 196 square feet

B. 49π square feet

C. 14π square feet

D. 7π square feet

29 Which expression can be used to find the missing values of $g(n)$ in the table below?

n	$g(n)$
1	1
3	7
5	13
6	16
7	?
8	?

A. $3n - 2$

B. $2n - 3$

C. $2n + 3$

D. $3n + 2$

30 Which set of lengths corresponds to a triangle similar to the one shown below?

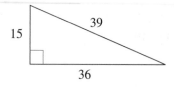

A. 4, 11, 12

B. 5, 12, 13

C. 6, 13, 14

D. 7, 14, 15

Question 31 is an open-response question.

- **BE SURE TO ANSWER AND LABEL ALL PARTS OF EACH QUESTION.**
- **Show all your work (diagrams, tables, or computations) in your Pretest Answer Booklet.**
- **If you do the work in your head, explain in writing how you did the work.**

Write your answer to question 31 in the space provided in your Pretest Answer Booklet.

31 Given points A, B, C and line segments $\overline{AB}$, $\overline{BC}$, $\overline{AC}$ in the figure below.

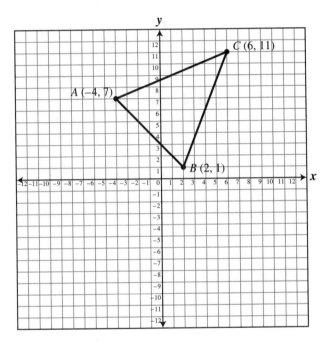

a. Calculate the length of $\overline{AB}$.

b. Determine the midpoint of $\overline{AB}$ and label it on the figure above as point D.

c. Calculate the area of $\triangle ABC$.

Mark your answers to multiple-choice questions 32 through 40 in the spaces provided in your Pretest Answer Booklet.

32 A cement drainage tunnel in the shape of a cylinder is being built under a road. If the length of the tunnel is 30 feet and the diameter is 6 feet, what is the surface area of the tunnel?

A. 66π

B. 78π

C. 180π

D. 198π

33 If the height of a regular pyramid is doubled, the volume of the pyramid is increased by a factor of

A. 5

B. 4

C. 3

D. 2

34 The median height of the players on a baseball team is 6 ft 1 in. What conclusion can be drawn?

A. The shortest player is 6 ft 1 in.

B. All players are taller then 6 ft 1 in.

C. The same number of players are taller than 6 ft 1 in. and shorter than 6 ft 1 in.

D. Most of the players are shorter than 6 ft 1 in. tall.

35 Delilah is planting a tulip garden consisting of red, lilac white, and yellow tulips. She really likes red tulips, so she plants twice as many red tulips as all of the other tulips combined. She decides to plant 5 each of the lilac white, and yellow tulips. All of the bulbs are placed in a basket. What is the probability that the first bulb she picks is a red bulb?

A. $\frac{2}{3}$

B. $\frac{2}{5}$

C. $\frac{1}{4}$

D. $\frac{1}{5}$

36 What is the value of the expression below?

$$\left(\frac{1}{3}\sqrt{81}\right)^3$$

A. 3

B. 9

C. 18

D. 27

37 The length of one base and one side of an isosceles trapezoid are shown below.

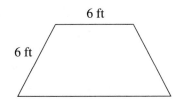

If the perimeter is 30 feet, what is the area?

A. 45 square feet

B. $27\sqrt{3}$ square feet

C. $54\sqrt{3}$ square feet

D. 36 square feet

Go
On

38 What is the value of the expression shown below?

$$\frac{z^2 - 6z + 9}{z^2 - 9} \div \frac{3z - 9}{z + 3}$$

A. $\frac{1}{3} \times \frac{(z - 3)}{(z + 3)}$

B. $\frac{1}{3}$

C. $\frac{3(z + 3)}{(z - 3)}$

D. 3

39 If 30 identical ball bearings weigh 50 grams, how many ball bearings weigh 200 grams?

A. 334

B. 210

C. 120

D. 333

40 The price per person to rent a limousine for a prom varies inversely as the number of passengers. If 6 people rent the limousine, the cost is $60 each. How many people are renting the limousine when the cost per person is $90?

A. 5

B. 4

C. 3

D. 2

Question 41 and 42 are open-response questions.

- **BE SURE TO ANSWER AND LABEL ALL PARTS OF EACH QUESTION.**
- **Show all your work (diagrams, tables, or computations) in your Pretest Answer Booklet.**
- **If you do the work in your head, explain in writing how you did the work.**

Write your answer to question 41 in the space provided in your Pretest Answer Booklet.

 Gracie has created a spreadsheet in which she has placed the powers of 3, 4, 5 and 6.

	A	B	C	D
1	3	4	5	6
2	9	16	25	36
3	27	64	125	216
4	81	256	625	1296
5				

a. What numbers will appear in row 5?

b. Gracie contends that any number that appears in column D is evenly divisible by the corresponding number in column A. Is she correct? Explain her reasoning.

42 The cost of a new violin made by a famous violin maker is $10,000. The violin increases in value by 10% in each of the first 3 years after the violin is made, then increases 5% per year after that. Write your answer to question 42 in the space provided in your Pretest Answer Booklet.

a. What is the value of the violin after 3 years?

b. What is the value of the violin after 4 years?

c. What is the earliest year in which the value of the violin has increased by at least 50% from its original price?

BE SURE YOU HAVE RECORDED ALL OF YOUR ANSWERS IN YOUR PRETEST ANSWER BOOKLET.

Lessons and Reviews

LESSON 1

NUMBER SENSE AND OPERATIONS

Learning Standards

10.N.1 *Identify and use the properties of operations on real numbers, including the associative, commutative, and distributive properties; the existence of the identity and inverse elements for addition and multiplication; the existence of nth roots of positive real numbers for any positive integer n; and the inverse relationship between taking the nth root of the nth power of a positive real number.*

10.N.2 *Simplify numerical expressions, including those involving positive integer exponents or the absolute value; apply such simplifications in the solution of problems.*

10.N.3 *Find the approximate value for solutions to problems involving square roots and cube roots without the use of a calculator.*

10.N.4 *Use estimation to judge the reasonableness of results of computations and of solutions to problems involving real numbers.*

What This Means

To answer questions assessed by these learning standards, you need to understand numbers, how numbers are represented, the relationships among numbers, and number systems. You must also understand the meaning of operations and how they relate to one another and be able to make reasonable estimates.

Properties

Some questions for these learning standards will involve properties. You will be asked to solve problems by selecting the correct property. *Properties* are characteristics describing the way operations—addition, subtraction, multiplication, and division—are performed. The following are some common properties:

Commutative Property of Addition and Multiplication

In addition and multiplication, numbers can be added in any order. For any real numbers $a + b$:

$$a + b = b + a \qquad a \times b = b \times a$$

Associative Property of Addition and Multiplication

For addition, add any two numbers together and then add the third. For any real numbers *a*, *b*, and *c*:

$$(a + b) + c = a + (b + c)$$

For multiplication, multiply two numbers and then multiple the product by the third number. For any real numbers *a*, *b*, and *c*:

$$(a \times b) \times c = a \times (b \times c)$$

Distributive Property

Multiplication is distributive over addition and subtraction. For any real numbers *a*, *b*, and *c*:

$$a (b + c) = ab + ac$$
$$a (b - c) = ab - ac$$

Order of Operations

To answer other questions assessed by these learning standards, you must know the correct order of operations for addition, subtraction, multiplication, and division. Follow these steps in this order:

1. If there are parentheses, do the operation within the parentheses first.

   $$(2 \times 3) \times 4$$
   $$6 \times 4 = 24$$

2. Next solve powers from left to right.

   $$3^2 + 9 + 2^2 = 9 + 9 + 4 = 18 + 4 = 22$$

3. Then solve multiplication and division in order from left to right.

   $$6 \times 3 + 4 \times 2 = 18 + 8 = 26$$

4. Finally solve addition and subtraction in order from left to right.

   $$6 + 3 - 5 = 9 - 5 = 4$$

Nth roots of Positive Real Numbers

You will also be asked to solve problems by identifying the *n*th root of a number. The *n*th root of a real number *x* is defined as a number that when multiplied by itself *n* times equals *x*.

The *n*th root of a number *x* is notated as: $\sqrt[n]{x}$

Example 1   The second or square root of 169 = 13 because 13 × 13 equals 169.

$$\sqrt{169} = 13 \text{ and } \sqrt{13^2} = 13$$

Example 2   The third or cube root of 8 = 2 because 2 times itself 3 times equals 8. In other words, 2 × 2 × 2 = 8.

$$\sqrt[3]{8} = 2 \text{ and } \sqrt[3]{2^3} = 2$$

Example 3   The fourth root of 81 = 3 because 3 times itself 4 times equals 81. In other words, 3 × 3 × 3 × 3 = 81.

$$\sqrt[4]{81} = 3 \text{ and } \sqrt[4]{3^4} = 3$$

Other Important Concepts

To answer questions for these learning skills, you should also know how to do the following:

- Convert decimals to fractions.
- Convert fractions to decimals.
- Find the square root of a number.
- Understand the difference between a rational number and an irrational number.
- Understand absolute value.

STEP ONE TEN-MINUTE LESSON

Sample Problem 1

The table below illustrates the Inverse Property for Multiplication. Given that the letters represent real numbers, what is the value of z?

	$\frac{1}{v}$	$\frac{1}{w}$	$\frac{1}{x}$	$\frac{1}{y}$
v	z	$\frac{v}{w}$	$\frac{v}{x}$	$\frac{v}{y}$
w	$\frac{w}{v}$	z	$\frac{w}{x}$	$\frac{w}{y}$
x	$\frac{x}{v}$	$\frac{x}{w}$	z	$\frac{x}{y}$
y	$\frac{y}{v}$	$\frac{y}{w}$	$\frac{y}{x}$	z

A. 0

B. $\frac{1}{2}$

C. $-\frac{1}{2}$

D. 1

Ⓐ   Ⓑ   Ⓒ   Ⓓ

Remember that the Inverse Property for Multiplication is the reciprocal of the number. Notice that z is only present in the cells of the table on the diagonal. In this table, these cells are located at positions (1, 1), (2, 2), (3, 3) and (4, 4). Calculate z by substituting small values for the variables. You may also calculate z from the variables themselves without substituting values.

For instance, to calculate z at cell (2, 2),

$$w \times \frac{1}{w} = \frac{w}{w} = 1$$

You will find that this holds true for all cells on the diagonal.

Therefore, $z = 1$.

Answer choice A: There aren't any numbers that you can substitute for *v*, *w*, *x*, and *y* that will produce a value of 0 for *z*, so this is not the correct answer choice. Also, you can't use 0 as a value because $\frac{1}{0}$ is undefined.

Answer choice B: This answer choice is also incorrect because there aren't any numbers that you can substitute for v, w, x, and y that will produce a value of $\frac{1}{2}$ for z.

Answer choice C: This answer choice is also incorrect. There aren't any numbers that you can substitute for *v*, *w*, *x*, and *y* that will produce a value of $-\frac{1}{2}$ for *z*.

Answer choice D: This is the correct answer choice. For any real number > 0 for *v*, *w*, *x*, and *y*, the value of *z* will always be 1.

Sample Problem 2

Sarah needed to determine the sum of three numbers: 1,234: 4,321: and 200. She followed these steps to find the answer:

Step 1   She calculated the sum of 4,321 and 200, which is 4,521.

Step 2   She calculated the sum of 1,234 and 4,521.

Which property do Sarah's calculations illustrate?

A. Distributive Property

B. Associative Property of Addition

C. Associative Property of Multiplication

D. Commutative Property of Addition

Ⓐ   Ⓑ   Ⓒ   Ⓓ

Answer choice A: The Distributive Property involves both addition and multiplication. Sarah did not use multiplication. This is not the correct answer choice.

Answer choice B: This is the correct answer choice. The Associative Property states that the grouping of the numbers doesn't matter. For example, 1,234 + (4,321 + 200) = (1,234 + 4,321) + 200. This illustrates Sarah's calculations. Even though this answer choice seems correct, always consider each answer choice before making a final decision.

Answer choice C: This answer choice is not correct because the Associative Property of Multiplication involves multiplication. Sarah did not use multiplication. This is not the correct answer choice.

Answer choice D: This answer choice is also incorrect because the Commutative Property states that the order of the numbers doesn't matter. For example, 1,234 + 4,321 + 200 = 200 + 4,321 + 1,234.

STEP TWO SIDEBAR INSTRUCTION

Complete the following problems. Use the Sidebar Instruction to help you choose the correct answer.

1 Which answer expresses the product $\sqrt{xy^3} \cdot \sqrt{xy^5}$ in its simplest form?

A. $16xy$

B. $x^2 y^8$

C. xy^4

D. xy^{15}

Ⓐ Ⓑ Ⓒ Ⓓ

SIDEBAR INSTRUCTION

For real numbers x and $y \geq 0$

$$\sqrt{x} \cdot \sqrt{y} = \sqrt{xy}$$

First, combine the x's and y's under the radical sign. Then apply the above rule to create nth roots of perfect squares. Lastly, simplify the nth roots.

2 What is the value of the following expression to the nearest tenth?

$$\sqrt{(-2)^3 (-1)^5 + (2)^1}$$

A. 3.1

B. 3.2

C. 3.3

D. 3.4

Ⓐ Ⓑ Ⓒ Ⓓ

SIDEBAR INSTRUCTION

This question asks you to find the square root of the expression under the radical sign. First, simplify the expression. Then find the perfect square closest to but *less* than the number under the radical sign, and the perfect square that is closest to but *more* than the number under the radical sign. Lastly, use the guess-and-check method to find the number that when multiplied by itself is closest to the value under the radical sign.

3 Which of the following is equivalent to the expression below?

$$3(6 - 2)^2 + 10|3 - 4| \times 10 \div 2$$

A. −2

B. 98

C. 194

D. 290

Ⓐ　Ⓑ　Ⓒ　Ⓓ

SIDEBAR INSTRUCTION

Expressions are always evaluated from left to right. Follow the order of operations as listed on page 26. Add and subtract in order from left to right. Remember that the result of an absolute value expression is *always* a positive number.

4 The population of the world is estimated at about 6,367,000,000. Which choice uses scientific notation for the estimated population?

A. stays the same

B. 6.4×10^{-4}

C. 6.367×10^9

D. 63.67×10^8

Ⓐ　Ⓑ　Ⓒ　Ⓓ

SIDEBAR INSTRUCTION

You need to understand scientific notation to correctly answer this question. To write a number in scientific notation, you first move the decimal point in the number to get a number between 1 and 10. Count how many places you move the decimal point. This is the power of 10.

Question 5 is an open-response question. Write your answers on the lines below.

5 Anna wants to evaluate the expressions 8(7.2 − 1.9).
To see whether her answer is reasonable. She first found
an approximate answer. Anna rounded each number within
parentheses to the nearest whole number.

SIDEBAR INSTRUCTION
Estimation is a way to
check whether an answer
is reasonable. Remember
to apply the order of
operations to both the
rounded numbers and the
exact numbers.

a. Evaluate the expression with these rounded numbers.

_____

b. What is the exact value of the expression?

_____

c. Which mathematical property does the expression illustrate?

_____

6 If $x^3 < x$, which of the following could be the value of x?

A. 3

B. 2

C. 0

D. $\dfrac{1}{2}$

Ⓐ   Ⓑ   Ⓒ   Ⓓ

7 Which of the following is equivalent to $\sqrt[4]{81n^4}$?

A. $9n^2$

B. $3n$

C. $3n^2$

D. $27n$

Ⓐ   Ⓑ   Ⓒ   Ⓓ

8 What is $\sqrt{\dfrac{1}{16}}$?

A. $\dfrac{1}{4}$

B. $\dfrac{1}{2}$

C. 4

D. 16

Ⓐ   Ⓑ   Ⓒ   Ⓓ

STEP THREE ON YOUR OWN

Complete each of the following problems. Choose the correct answer choice.

9 Which of the following is equivalent to the expression below?

$$2(4a + b) + 3(a + 2b) - 7(a - 3b)$$

A. $4ab$

B. $-4ab$

C. $4a + 29b$

D. $4a - 13b$

Ⓐ   Ⓑ   Ⓒ   Ⓓ

10 Ethan calculated the height of a wall as $\sqrt{100}$. Which of the following is equivalent to this value?

A. 50

B. $10\sqrt{10}$

C. 10

D. 10,000

Ⓐ   Ⓑ   Ⓒ   Ⓓ

11 Which of the following is the solution set for $|n - 5| = 4$?

A. $\{1\}$

B. $\{9\}$

C. $\{1, 9\}$

D. $\{-1, -9\}$

Ⓐ　Ⓑ　Ⓒ　Ⓓ

12 What is the value of the expression below?

$$5^0 + \sqrt{4^4}$$

A. 261

B. 256

C. 17

D. 16

Ⓐ　Ⓑ　Ⓒ　Ⓓ

13 What is the value of the following expression to the nearest tenth?

$\sqrt{23} \cdot 2$

A. 6.8

B. 8.6

C. 9.4

D. 9.6

Ⓐ   Ⓑ   Ⓒ   Ⓓ

14 Which choice shows the simplest form of $\sqrt[3]{x^{10}}$?

A. x^3

B. $x^3 \sqrt[3]{x}$

C. $\sqrt[3]{x^9} \cdot \sqrt[3]{x}$

D. $\dfrac{\sqrt[3]{x}}{2}$

Ⓐ   Ⓑ   Ⓒ   Ⓓ

15 Which expression simplifies the quotient of $\dfrac{7a^7b^4c^3}{21a^6b^2c^3d}$?

A. $\dfrac{ab^2}{3d}$

B. $\dfrac{a^{13}b^6c^6}{3d^3}$

C. $\dfrac{3a^2b}{d^3}$

D. $a^{13}b^6c^6$

Ⓐ   Ⓑ   Ⓒ   Ⓓ

16 $\sqrt[3]{125} + \sqrt[5]{+32}$

A. 7

B. 5

C. 4

D. 2

Ⓐ   Ⓑ   Ⓒ   Ⓓ

LESSON 2

MEASUREMENT

Learning Standards

10.M.1 *Calculate perimeter, circumference, and area of common geometric figures such as parallelograms, trapezoids, circles, and triangles.*

10.M.2 *Given the formula, find the lateral area, surface area, and volume of prisms, pyramids, spheres, cylinders, and cones; find the volume of a sphere with a specified surface area.*

10.M.3 *Relate changes in the measurement of one attribute of an object to changes in other attributes.*

10.M.4 *Describe the effects of approximate error in measurement and rounding on measurements and on computed values from measurements.*

What This Means

For these learning standards, you need to understand measurable attributes of objects and the units, systems, and processes of measurement. You will have to use the appropriate techniques, tools, and formulas to determine measurements.

For example, these types of questions may ask you to use and apply formulas for perimeter, area, and circumference to answer problems involving geometric shapes such as circles, squares, trapezoids, triangles, and parallelograms.

You will also be asked to apply formulas for surface area and volume to problems involving geometric solids such as prisms, pyramids, spheres, cylinders, and cones. You may also be asked to determine the effect of changing one attribute of an object on the other attributes of that object.

Important Concepts

You don't have to memorize the formulas needed to solve these problems. They will be given to you on a reference sheet. However, you need to know how to use these formulas correctly. You should be able to do the following:

- Find the circumference of a circle.

- Find the area of a circle.

- Find the area and perimeter of rectangles, parallelograms, and squares.

- Find the volume of a solid.

- Find the lateral area of a solid.

- Find the surface area of a solid.

STEP ONE TEN-MINUTE LESSON

Sample Problem 1

The square pyramid below has a base measuring 10 units and a height of 15 units.

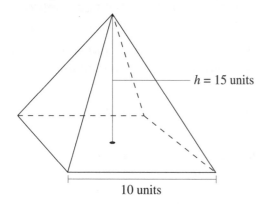

$h = 15$ units

10 units

What is the volume, in cubic units, of the pyramid?

A. 50 cubic units

B. 500 cubic units

C. 1,500 cubic units

D. 2,000 cubic units

Ⓐ   Ⓑ   Ⓒ   Ⓓ

To find the volume of the pyramid shown above, follow these steps.

Step 1   Determine the formula for the volume of a pyramid.

$V = \frac{1}{3} \times$ area of base $\times$ height

Step 2   Substitute the given values.

$V = \frac{1}{3} \times (10 \times 10) \times 15$

Step 3   Complete the operation.

$V = \frac{1}{3} \times 100 \times 15$

$V = \frac{1}{3} \times 1500$

$V = 500$

Step 4   Show the answer.

$V = 500$ cubic units

Answer choice A: This answer could not result from the application of the formula.

Answer choice B: This is the correct answer. It is the result of substituting the given value into the correct formula.

Answer choice C: This answer is not correct. It would result from applying $\frac{1}{2}$ instead of $\frac{1}{3}$ of the area of the base x the height.

Answer choice D: This answer is not correct. It is the result from applying the formula for finding the volume of a prism. (V_{prism} = area of base $\times$ height)

Sample Problem 2

If the area of a circular swimming pool is approximately 32 square feet, what is the approximate distance from the center of the pool to a side of the pool?

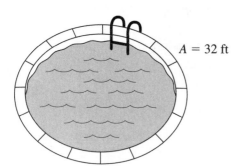

$A = 32$ ft

A. 0.98 ft

B. 3.19 ft

C. 1.60 ft

D. 10.19 ft

Ⓐ   Ⓑ   Ⓒ   Ⓓ

Since the swimming pool is circular in shape, the distance from the center of the swimming pool to the side of the pool is the length of the radius of the circle that the pool makes. You need to use the formula for the area of a circle that includes the radius.

Step 1   Determine the formula for the area of a circle.

$$A = \pi r^2$$

Step 2   Substitute the given value for area and solve for the radius.

Step 3   Solve.

$$32 = \pi \times r^2$$

$$r^2 = \frac{32}{\pi}$$

$$r = \sqrt{\frac{32}{\pi}}$$

$$r^2 = 10.19$$

Step 4   Show the answer.

Use 3.14 for π. Simplify.

$$r = \sqrt{10.19}$$

$$r \approx 3.19$$

Therefore, answer choice B is the correct answer.

Answer choice A: This answer is incorrect and may result from using an incorrect formula or an inaccurate computation.

Answer choice B: This is the correct answer choice. It is the result of using the correct formula for finding the area of a circle and performing the computations accurately.

Answer choice C: This is an incorrect answer. It could result if the formula for the area of a circle was erroneously thought to be $A = \pi d^2$.

Answer choice D: This answer is an incorrect answer. This answer could result if the formula for circumference of a circle $C = \pi d$ was used instead of the formula for the area of a circle.

STEP TWO | SIDEBAR INSTRUCTION

Complete the following problems. Use the Sidebar Instruction to help you choose the correct answer.

1 A regulation soccer ball has a circumference of approximately 28 inches. Which answer below is the best approximation of its surface area?

A. 1,018 square inches

B. 325 square inches

C. 250 square inches

D. 96 square inches

Ⓐ   Ⓑ   Ⓒ   Ⓓ

SIDEBAR INSTRUCTION

The formula for the surface area of a sphere is

$$SA = 4\pi r^2$$

where r is the radius of the circle.

Begin by finding the radius of the sphere. Remember that the definition of π is the circumference of a circle divided by the diameter, or $\pi = \frac{C}{d}$. Since the diameter equals 2 times the radius, rewrite the definition of π using the radius: $\pi = \frac{C}{2r}$. Substitute the circumference and solve for r. Then substitute r into the formula for surface area and solve.

Question 2 is a short-answer question. Write your answer on the lines below.

2 The inside of a cylindrical water tank must be coated to prevent the tank from rusting. If the height of the tank is 3 times the radius, and the radius of the tank is 2 feet, what is the surface area of the inside of the tank that must be covered to prevent the tank from rusting?

SIDEBAR INSTRUCTION

The formula for the surface area of a cylinder is

$$SA = 2\pi r^2 + 2\pi rh$$

where SA is the surface area, r is the radius, and h is the height. Since you know that the height is 3 times the radius, substitute $3r$ into the formula and simply.

$$SA = 2\pi r^2 + 2\pi r^3 r$$

$$SA = 2\pi r^2 + 6\pi r^2$$

$$SA = 8\pi r^2$$

Substitute the value for r into the formula $SA = 8\pi r^2$ and solve for SA.

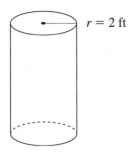

$r = 2$ ft

_____

_____

_____

3 The radius of a cylinder is increased by a factor of 3. What is the effect on the volume of a cylinder?

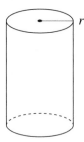

A. The volume is increased by a factor of 12.

B. The volume is increased by a factor of 9.

C. The volume is increased by a factor of 6.

D. The volume is increased by a factor of 3.

Ⓐ   Ⓑ   Ⓒ   Ⓓ

SIDEBAR INSTRUCTION

The formula for the volume of a cylinder is

$$V = \pi r^2 h$$

where V is the volume of the cylinder, r is the radius and h is the height.

Begin by increasing the radius by a factor of 3, which will make the radius equal $3 \times r$ or $3r$. Then substitute $3r$ into the formula and simplify. Then compare the formulas for the old and new volumes.

4 The height of a cone is 9 inches, and the diameter of the opening is 7 inches. What is the approximate volume of the cone?

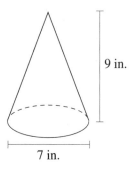

9 in.

7 in.

A. 115 cubic inches

B. 346 cubic inches

C. 462 cubic inches

D. 1,385 cubic inches

Ⓐ   Ⓑ   Ⓒ   Ⓓ

SIDEBAR INSTRUCTION

The formula for the volume of a cone is

$$V = \frac{1}{3}\pi r^2 h$$

where V is the volume of a cone, r is the radius, and h is the height.

Recall that the diameter is 2 times the radius, so the radius is $\frac{1}{2}$ of the diameter. Calculate the value of the radius. Substitute it into the formula and solve.

5 Phillip is buying a new hot-water tank for his house. The current tank has a diameter of 2 feet and is 3 feet tall. If the new tank has the same diameter as the old one, what must be true of the new tank for it to be double the capacity of the old tank?

A. The new tank must be four times as tall as the old tank.

B. The new tank must be $\frac{2}{3}$ the height of the old tank.

C. The new tank must be twice as tall as the old tank.

D. The new tank must be the same height as the old tank.

Ⓐ   Ⓑ   Ⓒ   Ⓓ

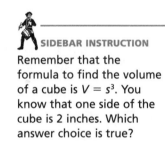

SIDEBAR INSTRUCTION
Remember that the diameter is the same for both tanks. Therefore, what must change in order for it to hold twice the amount of the first tank?

6 If an edge of a cube is decreased from 4 inches to 2 inches, what will be the effect on the volume of the cube?

A. The volume will be increased by a factor of 4.

B. The volume will be increased by a factor of 8.

C. The volume will be reduced by a factor of 64.

D. The volume will be reduced by a factor of 8.

Ⓐ   Ⓑ   Ⓒ   Ⓓ

SIDEBAR INSTRUCTION
Remember that the formula to find the volume of a cube is $V = s^3$. You know that one side of the cube is 2 inches. Which answer choice is true?

STEP THREE **ON YOUR OWN**

Complete the following problems. Choose the correct answer choice.

7 Roger and his father are planting grass in a new park in their neighborhood. They're using Roger's father's truck to haul topsoil.

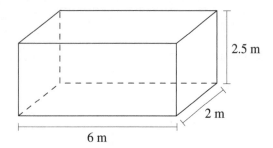

2.5 m

2 m

6 m

The truck bed is 6 meters long, 2 meters wide and 2.5 meters high. What is the total volume of the truck bed in cubic meters?

A. 30 cubic meters

B. 45 cubic meters

C. 60 cubic meters

D. 72 cubic meters

Ⓐ   Ⓑ   Ⓒ   Ⓓ

8 Ray has a circular above-ground swimming pool whose diameter is 10 feet. If he replaces this pool with a new one measuring 16 feet in diameter, what is the increase in the area taken up by the pool?

A. 39π

B. 64π

C. 128π

D. 156π

Ⓐ   Ⓑ   Ⓒ   Ⓓ

9 A cube has a surface area of 21,600 square units. What is the length of one edge of the cube?

A. 45

B. 60

C. 73

D. 90

Ⓐ Ⓑ Ⓒ Ⓓ

Question 10 is a short-answer question. Write your answer on the lines below.

10 The area of the trapezoid below is 408 units. The sum of the bases is 48 units. What is the height of the trapezoid?

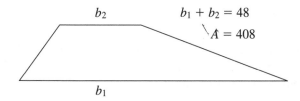

_____

_____

11 One of the two equal sides of an isosceles triangle is 10 units, while the perimeter of the triangle is 32 units. What is the area of the triangle?

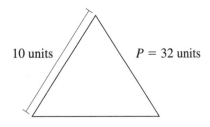

10 units $P = 32$ units

A. 48 square units

B. 56 square units

C. 76 square units

D. 96 square units

Ⓐ   Ⓑ   Ⓒ   Ⓓ

12 Package designers are developing a new package for 6 pieces of chalk that each measure 3 inches in height and 1 inch in diameter. In square inches, what is the total surface area of these 6 pieces of chalk?

A. 10.5π

B. 21π

C. 36π

D. 48π

Ⓐ   Ⓑ   Ⓒ   Ⓓ

13 The height of a rectangular box is 2 inches, and the length of the box is twice as long as the width. If the volume of the box is 196 cubic inches, what are the values of the length and width of the box?

A. width = 7, length = 14

B. width = 4, length = 8

C. width = 14, length = 7

D. width = 10, length = 20

Ⓐ   Ⓑ   Ⓒ   Ⓓ

REVIEW 1

This section reviews the learning standards in Lessons 1 and 2. Answer each of the following questions.

1 What is the $\sqrt{7^2}$?

A. 7

B. 14

C. 49

D. 98

Ⓐ Ⓑ Ⓒ Ⓓ

2 The length of Alex's swimming pool is $2\sqrt{144}$. Which answer choice is another way to express this distance?

A. 24

B. 48

C. 72

D. 144

Ⓐ Ⓑ Ⓒ Ⓓ

3 Joelle is the manager of inventory for frozen yogurt stands in her city. Using *a* to represent strawberry yogurt, *b* to represent peach yogurt, and *c* to represent blueberry yogurt, Joelle needs to find the amount of yogurt in stock. Which expression represents the inventory of all three stands?

Stand 1

$$5a - 2b + 14c$$

Stand 2

$$2a + 7b - 3c$$

Stand 3

$$10a + 12b + 5c$$

A. $7a - 21b - 22c$

B. $17a + 17b + 16c$

C. $17a - 15b - 16c$

D. $100a - 168b - 615c$

Ⓐ　Ⓑ　Ⓒ　Ⓓ

4 Which of the following is equivalent to the expression below?

$$3(6 - 2)^2 + 10(3 + 4) \times 10 \div 2$$

A. 123

B. 398

C. 485

D. 590

Ⓐ　Ⓑ　Ⓒ　Ⓓ

Question 5 is a short-answer question. Write your answer on the lines below.

5   An oil company stores oil in two vats: A large vat which has a diameter of 10 feet and a height of 12 feet, and a small vat which has a diameter of 4 feet and a height of 6 feet. How much more oil can be stored in the large vat than the small vat?

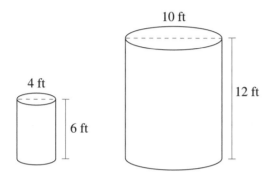

_____

_____

6 The length of one base, one side, and the height of an isosceles trapezoid are shown below.

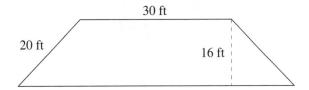

What is the area of the figure?

A. 244 square feet

B. 432 square feet

C. 480 square feet

D. 672 square feet

Ⓐ   Ⓑ   Ⓒ   Ⓓ

7 The circumference of a circle is 50π feet. After the circle is dilated the area of the new circle is 25π square feet. What is the scale factor?

A. $\dfrac{1}{5}$

B. $\dfrac{1}{2}$

C. 5

D. 10

Ⓐ   Ⓑ   Ⓒ   Ⓓ

8 The Hot Stuff Spice Company packages its product in cube-shaped boxes whose sides each measure 3 inches. The spices are shipped to wholesalers in a packing crate that is 36 inches wide, 18 inches deep, and 12 inches high. What is the greatest number of spice boxes that will fit in a packing crate?

A. 72 boxes

B. 288 boxes

C. 384 boxes

D. 1,152 boxes

Ⓐ Ⓑ Ⓒ Ⓓ

9 What is the value of 11 + 3 × 2?

A. 16

B. 17

C. 26

D. 28

Ⓐ Ⓑ Ⓒ Ⓓ

10 Which has the greatest value?

A. $\dfrac{1}{4}$

B. $\left(\dfrac{1}{4}\right)^2$

C. $\left(\dfrac{1}{4}\right)^3$

D. $\sqrt{\dfrac{1}{4}}$

Ⓐ   Ⓑ   Ⓒ   Ⓓ

LESSON 3

Learning Standards

10.G.1 *Identify figures using properties of sides, angles, and diagonals. Identify the figures' type(s) of symmetry.*

10.G.2. *Draw congruent and similar figures using a compass, straightedge, protractor, and other tools such as computer software. Make conjectures about methods of construction. Justify the conjectures by logical arguments.*

10.G.3 *Recognize and solve problems involving angles formed by transversals of coplanar lines. Identify and determine the measure of central and inscribed angles and their associated minor and major arcs. Recognize and solve problems associated with radii, chords, arcs within or on the same circle.*

10.G.4 *Apply congruence and similarity correspondences and properties of the figures to find missing parts of geometric figures, and provide logical justification.*

10.G.5 *Solve simple triangle problems using the triangle angle sum property and/or the Pythagorean theorem.*

10.G.6 *Use the properties of special triangles to solve problems.*

What This Means

Questions for these learning standards will ask you to analyze the characteristics and properties of two- and three-dimensional geometric shapes and develop mathematical arguments about geometric relationships. They might ask you to specify locations and describe spatial relationships using coordinate geometry. You may be asked to identify a figure's line(s) of symmetry. You may be asked to apply transformations and use symmetry to analyze mathematical situations and use visualization, spatial reasoning, and geometric modeling to solve problems.

You may also be asked to solve problems in circle geometry, such as measuring central and inscribed angles and their corresponding arcs, as well as problems involving the radii and chords of a circle. In addition, you can expect to be asked to use the concepts of congruence and similarity to find missing parts of geometric figures.

You don't have to memorize formulas to answer these questions. These formulas will be given to you on a reference sheet.

Important Concepts

You should be familiar with the following geometric concepts:

- Lines and angles
- Angles formed by transversals
- Lines intersecting parallel lines and angles formed by these lines
- Polygons
- Triangles
- Chords and arcs of circles
- Congruence and similarity
- Triangle angle sum property
- Pythagorean theorem

STEP ONE TEN-MINUTE LESSON

Sample Problem 1

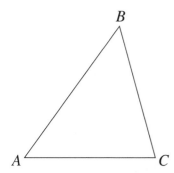

The triangle above can best be described as what type of triangle?

A. right

B. equilateral

C. scalene

D. isosceles

Ⓐ   Ⓑ   Ⓒ   Ⓓ

Answer Choice A: A right triangle contains a 90-degree angle. Since this triangle does not, this answer choice is incorrect.

Answer Choice B: The measures of each of the three sides of an equilateral triangle are equal. Since each side of the $\triangle ABC$ has a different measure, this answer choice is incorrect.

Answer Choice C: A scalene triangle is one in which each side has a different measure. This triangle is a scalene triangle. Therefore, this answer choice is correct.

Answer Choice D: An isosceles triangle has two sides that have equal measure. This triangle does not. This answer choice is incorrect.

Sample Problem 2

In the figure below, how many lines of symmetry are there, and what are their equations?

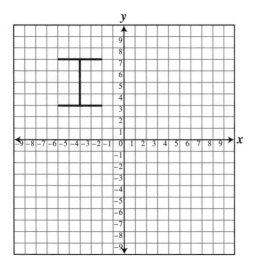

A. none

B. 1 line of symmetry, equation is $y = -5$

C. 2 lines of symmetry, equations are $x = -4$, $y = 5$

D. 2 lines of symmetry, equations are $x = 5$, $y = -4$

Ⓐ   Ⓑ   Ⓒ   Ⓓ

You can usually "see" a line of symmetry in a figure as a line that cuts the figure in half so that the pieces are identical in shape and size. To check a line of symmetry, pick a point on the figure and count the number of squares from that point to the line of symmetry. If a point exists on the graph that is exactly the same distance from the line but on the other side, then it IS a line of symmetry.

This figure looks like it has a vertical line of symmetry along the line $x = -4$.

Pick the point on the graph $(-6, 7)$ and count the number of squares to the line (2). Now count 2 squares from the line in the same direction and you get a point on the graph on the other side of the line. So the equation of a line of symmetry is $x = -4$.

It also looks as if there's a line of symmetry at $y = 5$. Using the same test as before, you can see that $y = 5$ also cuts the figure equally into two pieces.

So there are two lines of symmetry and the equations are $x = -4$ and $y = 5$. Answer choice C is the correct answer.

STEP TWO SIDEBAR INSTRUCTION

Complete the following problems. Use the Sidebar Instruction to help you choose the correct answer.

1 Which of the following pairs of angles in the figure below are congruent?

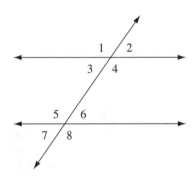

A. $\angle 3$ and $\angle 5$

B. $\angle 3$ and $\angle 6$

C. $\angle 1$ and $\angle 2$

D. $\angle 6$ and $\angle 8$

Ⓐ   Ⓑ   Ⓒ   Ⓓ

 SIDEBAR INSTRUCTION

When two parallel lines are cut by a transversal, the following statements are true. (1) Alternate interior angles are congruent. These angles are on opposite sides of the transversal between the parallel lines. (2) Corresponding angles are congruent. These angles are on the same side of the transversal where one of the angles is outside the parallel lines and the other angle is between them. Choose the answer choice that best satisfies these conditions.

2 What is the area of the square below?

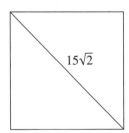

$15\sqrt{2}$

A. 225

B. 175

C. 112.5

D. 60

Ⓐ   Ⓑ   Ⓒ   Ⓓ

SIDEBAR INSTRUCTION

Since the figure is a square, the diagonal forms two 45°–45°–90° triangles. Use the Pythagorean theorem to find the measure of each side of the square. Then calculate the area.

Question 3 is an open-response question. Write your answer on the lines below.

3   In the triangle below, the measures of $\overline{AB}$ and $\overline{CB}$ are equal.

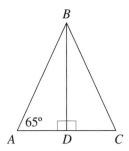

a.   What is the measure of $\angle ABD$?

_____

SIDEBAR INSTRUCTION

Since $\angle ADB$ is a right angle, use the triangle angle sum property to find the measure of $\angle ABD$.

b.   What is the measure of $\angle CBD$?

_____

SIDEBAR INSTRUCTION

Since the measures of $\overline{AB}$ and $\overline{CB}$ are equal, then $\triangle ABC$ is an isosceles triangle, and $\overline{BD}$ forms two congruent triangles: $\triangle ABD$ and $\triangle CBD$. Use the fact that corresponding parts of congruent triangles are congruent to find the measure of $\angle CBD$.

4 In the figures below, △*ABC* is similar to △*DEF*. What is the measure of *EF*?

SIDEBAR INSTRUCTION

In similar triangles, corresponding parts are proportional. So

$$\frac{AC}{DF} = \frac{BC}{EF}$$

Substitute the known values into the equation and solve for *EF*.

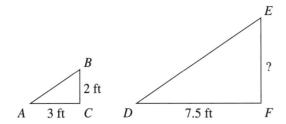

A. 0.8 ft

B. 5 ft

C. 10 ft

D. 12.5 ft

Ⓐ Ⓑ Ⓒ Ⓓ

5 The measure of minor arc $\widehat{AB} = 70°$. What is the measure of ∠*ACB*?

SIDEBAR INSTRUCTION

Use the fact that the measure of an angle inscribed in a circle equals one-half the measure of the intercepted arc.

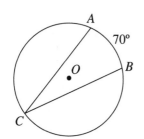

A. 70°

B. 60°

C. 45°

D. 35°

Ⓐ Ⓑ Ⓒ Ⓓ

6   In right △*ABC*, the measures of ∠*A* and ∠*C* are equal. Find $\overline{AC}$ if $\overline{AB}$ equals $\sqrt{2}$.

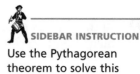

SIDEBAR INSTRUCTION

Use the Pythagorean theorem to solve this problem.

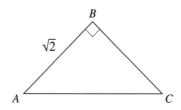

A. $\sqrt{2}$

B. 2

C. $\sqrt{5}$

D. 4

Ⓐ   Ⓑ   Ⓒ   Ⓓ

7   Which triangle is NOT similar to the triangle shown below?

SIDEBAR INSTRUCTION

Remember that two triangles are similar if any two angles of one triangle are congruent to two angles of the other triangle or the sides of one triangle are proportional to the sides of the other triangle.

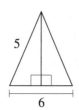

5

6

A.

9   6

C.

60

48

B.

15

34

D.

15

18

Ⓐ   Ⓑ   Ⓒ   Ⓓ

8 The figure below is of a right triangle.

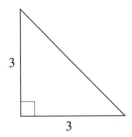

SIDEBAR INSTRUCTION
Use the Pythagorean theorem to find the length of the triangle's hypotenuse: $a^2 + b^2 = c^2$.

What is the length of the hypotenuse? Round your answer to the nearest tenth.

A. 2.4

B. 4.2

C. 5.2

D. 18.0

Ⓐ   Ⓑ   Ⓒ   Ⓓ

STEP THREE **ON YOUR OWN**

Complete the following problems. Choose the correct answer choice.

9 Lines $\overline{AB}$ and $\overline{CD}$ are parallel. What is the measure of $\angle BCD$?

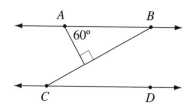

A. 60°

B. 45°

C. 30°

D. 15°

Ⓐ Ⓑ Ⓒ Ⓓ

10 Identify the line of symmetry in the figure below.

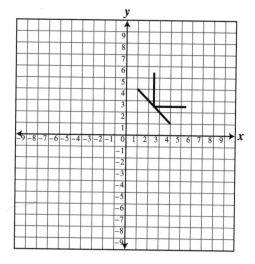

A. $y = -x$

B. $y = x$

C. $x = 5$

D. $y = 5$

Ⓐ Ⓑ Ⓒ Ⓓ

11 The measure of minor arc $\overarc{AB} = 120°$. What is the measure of $\angle BAC$?

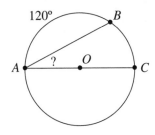

A. 75°

B. 60°

C. 30°

D. 15°

Ⓐ   Ⓑ   Ⓒ   Ⓓ

12 What is the approximate area of the rectangle below?

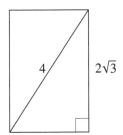

A. 14 square units

B. 7 square units

C. 5 square units

D. 4 square units

Ⓐ   Ⓑ   Ⓒ   Ⓓ

13 Claude wants to build a triangular-shaped swimming pool in his backyard. He has drawn a scale model where the lengths of the sides are 5, 12 and 13 inches, respectively. If the longest side of the pool will be 39 feet, what will be the lengths of the other two sides?

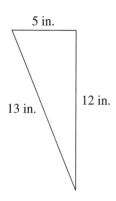

A. 48 feet, 20 feet

B. 24 feet, 10 feet

C. 36 feet, 15 feet

D. 30 feet, 12.5 feet

Ⓐ   Ⓑ   Ⓒ   Ⓓ

14 What is the measure of $\angle C$?

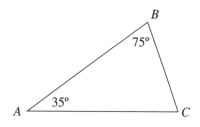

A. 35°

B. 70°

C. 75°

D. 90°

Ⓐ   Ⓑ   Ⓒ   Ⓓ

15 In the figure below, lines *x* and *y* are parallel. Angle 1 is 130°. What other angle is 130°?

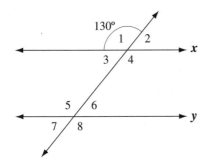

A. ∠2

B. ∠3

C. ∠6

D. ∠8

Ⓐ   Ⓑ   Ⓒ   Ⓓ

16 What is the measure of ∠*x*?

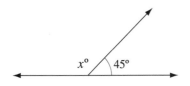

A. 45°

B. 90°

C. 120°

D. 135°

Ⓐ   Ⓑ   Ⓒ   Ⓓ

Question 17 is a short-answer question. Write your answer on the lines below.

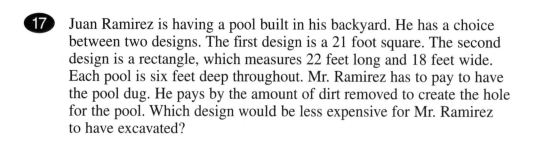

17 Juan Ramirez is having a pool built in his backyard. He has a choice between two designs. The first design is a 21 foot square. The second design is a rectangle, which measures 22 feet long and 18 feet wide. Each pool is six feet deep throughout. Mr. Ramirez has to pay to have the pool dug. He pays by the amount of dirt removed to create the hole for the pool. Which design would be less expensive for Mr. Ramirez to have excavated?

_____

_____

LESSON 4

GEOMETRY, PART 2

Learning Standards

10.G.7 *Using rectangular coordinates, calculate midpoints of segments, slopes of lines and segments, and distances between points, and apply the results to the solutions of problems.*

10.G.8 *Find linear equations that represent lines either perpendicular or parallel to a given line and through a point.*

10.G.9 *Draw the results, and interpret transformations on figures in the coordinate plane. Apply transformations to the solutions of problems.*

10.G.10 *Demonstrate the ability to visualize solid objects and recognize their projections and cross sections.*

10.G.11 *Use vertex-edge graphs to model and solve problems.*

What This Means

Questions based on these learning standards use the *x-y* coordinate plane to describe geometric objects.

You may be asked to calculate the distance between points or the slope of a line. You may be required to find the equation of a line or the equation of a line that is parallel or perpendicular to a given line passing through a particular point. In addition, you might also be asked to interpret transformations such as translations, rotations, and reflections on geometric objects.

Some questions might ask you to visualize what a solid object looks like from a flat pattern, called a *net*.

Important Concepts

- Transformations on the coordinate plane (translation, rotation, and reflection)

- Properties of solid objects (two- and three-dimensional)

- Linear equations

- Slope of parallel and perpendicular lines

- Distance between points

- Lines of symmetry

STEP ONE TEN-MINUTE LESSON

Sample Problem 1

The line in the grid below passes through points (2, 5) and (10, 9).
What is the slope of this line?

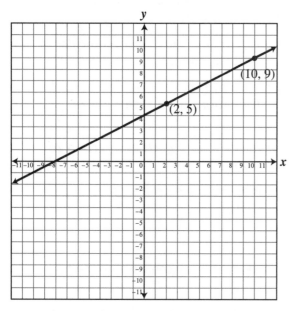

A. $\dfrac{1}{2}$ C. 2

B. $-\dfrac{1}{2}$ D. $\dfrac{2}{3}$

Ⓐ   Ⓑ   Ⓒ   Ⓓ

Answer choice A: This is the correct answer. It resulted from forming a fraction where the numerator is the difference in the *y* values and the denominator is the difference in the *x* values taken in the same order.

Answer choice B: This choice is incorrect. If you subtract using an inconsistent order, for example $\dfrac{9-5}{2-10}$, you get $-\dfrac{1}{2}$.

Answer choice C: This choice is incorrect. The answer could result from mistakenly trying to find the slope using $\dfrac{\text{the difference in } x}{\text{the difference in } y}$.

Answer choice D: This choice is incorrect and might result from improperly finding the difference between the given integers.

72

Sample Problem 2

What is the approximate distance between the two points shown on the grid below?

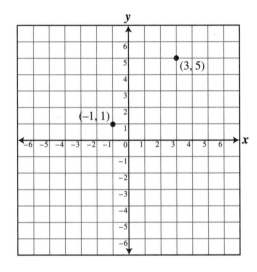

A. 4.5

B. 5.7

C. 7.2

D. 16.0

Ⓐ   Ⓑ   Ⓒ   Ⓓ

$$d = \sqrt{(x_2 - x_1)^2 + (y_2 - y_1)^2}$$

$$= \sqrt{(3 - (-1))^2 + (5 - 1)^2}$$

$$= \sqrt{16 + 16}$$

$$= \sqrt{32}$$

$$\approx 5.7$$

Answer choice A: This choice is incorrect. It could result from improper substitution, inaccurate combination of integers, or an inability to find the square root of a number.

Answer choice B: This is the correct answer. It results from consistent substitution into the distance fromula and accurate work with integers and finding the square root correctly.

Answer choice C: This choice is incorrect. It could result from inaccurate combining of integers.

Answer choice D: This choice is incorrect. It could result from not being able to accurately find the square root of a number.

STEP TWO SIDEBAR INSTRUCTION

Complete the following problems. Use the Sidebar Instruction to help you choose the correct answer.

1 What is the midpoint of line segment $\overline{AB}$?

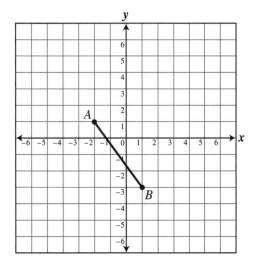

SIDEBAR INSTRUCTION

The formula for the midpoint of a line segment with endpoints

(x_1, y_1) and (x_2, y_2) is

$\left(\dfrac{(x_1 + x_2)}{2}, \dfrac{(y_1 + y_2)}{2}\right)$

Determine the coordinates from the graph. Then substitute them into the formula to find the answer.

A. $(-1, -\dfrac{1}{2})$

B. $(-\dfrac{1}{2}, -1)$

C. $(1, \dfrac{1}{2})$

D. $(\dfrac{1}{2}, 1)$

Ⓐ   Ⓑ   Ⓒ   Ⓓ

2 Which of the equations below describes a line that passes through the point (2, 5) and is perpendicular to the line $y - \frac{1}{2}x = 4$?

A. $y = 2x + 12$

B. $y = -2x + 9$

C. $y = \frac{1}{2}x + 12$

D. $y = -\frac{1}{2}x + 9$

Ⓐ   Ⓑ   Ⓒ   Ⓓ

SIDEBAR INSTRUCTION

The slopes of perpendicular lines are negative reciprocals of each other. To solve this problem, (1) Put the equation in *y*-intercept form.

$y = \frac{1}{2}x + 4$

(2) Look at the slope of the given line. Write an equation with a slope that is the negative reciprocal of the slope of the given equation with a variable for the unknown constant. (3) A perpendicular line to the given line must have slope of -2. Find the constant for the equation in Step 2 by substituting the coordinates into the new equation and solve the constant. (4) Substitute point (2, 5) into new equation to make sure line passes through the point.

3 Look at the figure below. If a new rectangle $A'B'C'D'$ was formed under a translation of $(-2, 4)$, what would be the coordinates of D'?

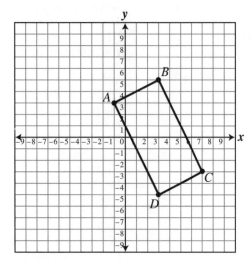

A. $(-1, 1)$

B. $(7, -7)$

C. $(-7, 7)$

D. $(1, -1)$

Ⓐ Ⓑ Ⓒ Ⓓ

4 Daryl bought a desk with a right-hand return to use in his home office. He originally intended to position it as shown in the grid below. Due to the shape of his office, Daryl must rotate the desk 90 degrees in a counterclockwise direction about the origin. What will be the new position of point *E* on the grid after the rotation?

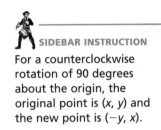

SIDEBAR INSTRUCTION

For a counterclockwise rotation of 90 degrees about the origin, the original point is (*x*, *y*) and the new point is (−*y*, *x*).

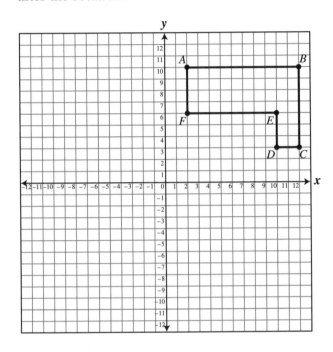

A. (6, −10)

B (2, 14)

C. (−6, 10)

D. (14, 2)

Ⓐ Ⓑ Ⓒ Ⓓ

5 What is the slope of line *m*?

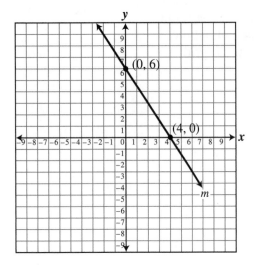

SIDEBAR INSTRUCTION

Remember that when a line is rising from left to right, the slope is positive. When the line is falling from left to right the slope is negative. Since the line is falling, the slope is negative, so eliminate choices A and D.

A. $\frac{2}{3}$

B. $-\frac{2}{3}$

C. $-\frac{3}{2}$

D. $\frac{3}{2}$

Ⓐ   Ⓑ   Ⓒ   Ⓓ

6 If figure *ABCD* is reflected over the *x*-axis, what are the coordinates of point *C*?

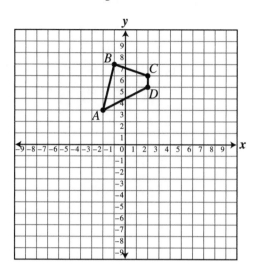

A. (2, −5)

B. (2, −6)

C. (−2, −3)

D. (−1, −7)

Ⓐ   Ⓑ   Ⓒ   Ⓓ

STEP THREE ON YOUR OWN

Complete the following problems. Choose the correct answer choice.

7 Which of the following is an equation for a line that is NOT parallel to
$-x + 2y - 4 = 0$

A. $y = \dfrac{1}{2}x - 1$

B. $y = \dfrac{1}{2}x + 21$

C. $-x + 2y + 4 = 0$

D. $-2x + 2y - 4 = 0$

Ⓐ   Ⓑ   Ⓒ   Ⓓ

8 A straight line passes through the points $(-5, 4)$ and $(5, -2)$.

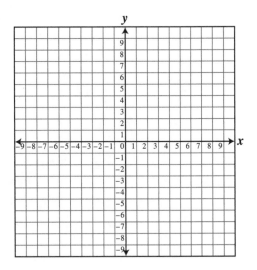

a. Label the points and plot this line on the graph above.
    List two other coordinates of this line.

_____

b. What is the slope of this line?

_____

9 Which pair of coordinates would be included on a line of symmetry for the figure below?

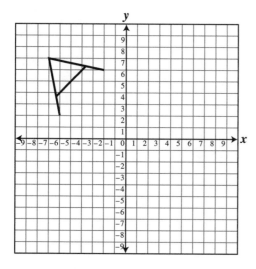

A. (2, −2)

B. (−2, −2)

C. (−1, 2)

D. (1, −2)

Ⓐ   Ⓑ   Ⓒ   Ⓓ

10 Maria and her class plan to build a platform for an upcoming show. In the scale model of the platform, the length is 10 inches and the width is 5 inches.

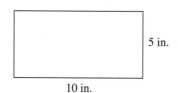

5 in.

10 in.

If the width of the full-size platform will be 15 feet, what will be the length of the platform?

A. 15 feet

B. 20 feet

C. 30 feet

D. 35 feet

Ⓐ   Ⓑ   Ⓒ   Ⓓ

11 The data below describe two lines in the coordinate plane.

x	y
4	2
6	4
8	6
10	8

x	y
0	0
−2	2
−4	4
−6	6

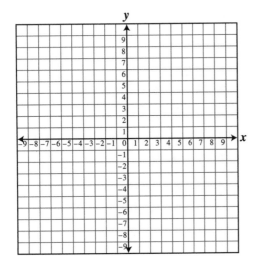

In which quadrant is the point of intersection?

A. Quadrant I

B. Quadrant II

C. Quadrant III

D. Quadrant IV

Ⓐ   Ⓑ   Ⓒ   Ⓓ

12 Which illustration is a net for a cylinder?

A.

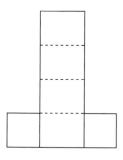

C.

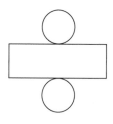

B.

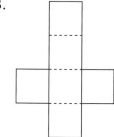

D.

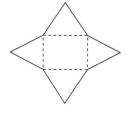

Ⓐ Ⓑ Ⓒ Ⓓ

13 What is the volume, in cubic units, of the figure below?

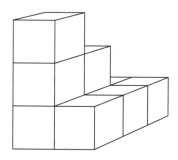

A. 3

B. 6

C. 9

D. 10

Ⓐ Ⓑ Ⓒ Ⓓ

14 Which of the following is a true statement about the net of the object shown?

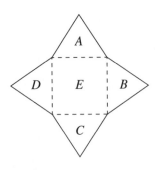

A. Faces *A* and *C* are parallel.

B. Faces *E* and *C* are perpendicular.

C. Faces *A* and *D* are adjacent.

D. Faces *A* and *E* are perpendicular.

Ⓐ   Ⓑ   Ⓒ   Ⓓ

REVIEW 2

This section reviews the learning standards in Lessons 3 and 4. Complete each of the following problems. Choose the correct answer choice.

1 The layout of a park calls for a reflection of fountain *ABCD* to the opposite side of a stream to create a second fountain *A'B'C'D'*. The fountain and the stream are depicted in the graph below.

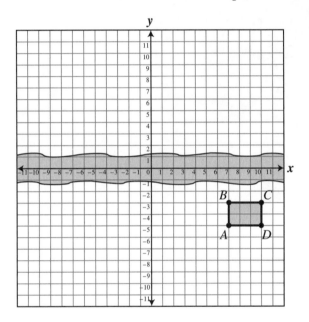

What are the coordinates of point *C'* after the reflection?

A. (7, 6)

B. (10, 3)

C. (7, 3)

D. (10, 6)

Ⓐ   Ⓑ   Ⓒ   Ⓓ

Question 2 is a short-answer question. Write your answer on the line below.

2   A suspension bridge is supported by wires coming from the middle of a tall pole down to the ground. These wires are 100 feet long and are attached to the ground at a distance of 30 feet from the pole. The top of the pole is how high above the bridge's roadway? Round your answer to the nearest whole number.

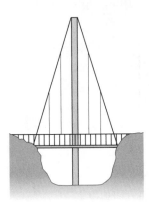

_____

3 Adelia and her family traveled to Maitland to work as volunteers for the Save the Manatee Club. Adelia is drawing a large map to show the class the distance from their school, which is near Key Largo, to Maitland. She uses 2 centimeters to represent 100 miles. What is the approximate distance from Key Largo to Maitland if Adelia's map represents the distance as 7 centimeters?

A. 14 miles

B. 200 miles

C. 350 miles

D. 400 miles

Ⓐ Ⓑ Ⓒ Ⓓ

4 In the diagram below, what is the measure of ∠6?

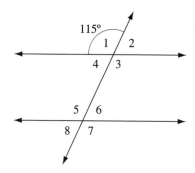

A. 45°

B. 65°

C. 115°

D. 125°

Ⓐ Ⓑ Ⓒ Ⓓ

5 The measure of minor arc $\overset{\frown}{AB} = 110°$. What is the measure of $\angle BOC$?

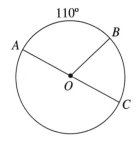

A. 45°

B. 55°

C. 70°

D. 115°

Ⓐ   Ⓑ   Ⓒ   Ⓓ

6 If △*ABC* is translated so that point *C'* has coordinates (−2, −1), what will be the new coordinates of point *B'*?

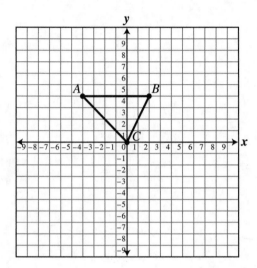

A. (3, 0)

B. (1, −1)

C. (3, −6)

D. (0, 3)

Ⓐ Ⓑ Ⓒ Ⓓ

7 In the diagram below line segments $\overline{AB}$ and $\overline{CD}$ are parallel. Line $\overline{EF}$ is perpendicular to AB. Line GH bisects $\angle CJF$. How many degrees are there in $\angle HKB$?

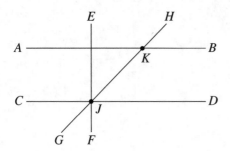

A. 30°

B. 45°

C. 60°

D. 90°

ⓐ   ⓑ   ⓒ   ⓓ

8 What is the equation of a line that is perpendicular to the line $-5x + y = 12$?

A. $y = 5x + 12$

B. $y = \dfrac{x}{5} + 12$

C. $-y = -5x + 7$

D. $y = -\dfrac{x}{5} + 6$

ⓐ   ⓑ   ⓒ   ⓓ

9 In the graph below, point A corresponds to point A_1, point B corresponds to point B_1 and point C corresponds to point C_1. What must the coordinates be for point B_1 so that $\triangle A_1B_1C_1$ is similar to $\triangle ABC$?

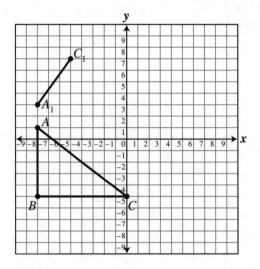

A. $(3, -5)$

B. $(-10, -3)$

C. $(-5, 3)$

D. $(-8, -6)$

Ⓐ   Ⓑ   Ⓒ   Ⓓ

Question 10 is a short-answer question. Write your answer on the lines below.

10 Straight line *M* passes through the points $(-1, 2)$ and $(2, 5)$.
Straight line *N* passes through the points $(-1, 4)$ and $(1, 2)$.

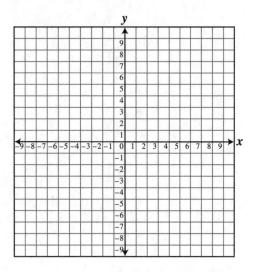

a. Label the points above and plot these two lines on the graph.
List two other coordinates of each of these lines.

_____

b. What are the slopes of each line?

_____

LESSON 5

PATTERNS, RELATIONS, AND ALGEBRA, PART 1

Learning Standards

10.P.1 *Describe, complete, extend, analyze, generalize, and create a wide variety of patterns, including iterative, recursive, linear, quadratic, and exponential functional relationships.*

10.P.2 *Demonstrate an understanding of the relationship between various representations of a line. Determine a line's slope and x- and y-intercepts from its graph or from a linear equation that represents the line. Find a linear equation describing a line from a graph or a geometric description of the line.*

10.P.3 *Add, subtract, and multiply polynomials. Divide polynomials by monomials.*

10.P.4 *Demonstrate facility in symbolic manipulation of polynomial and rational expressions by rearranging and collecting terms, factoring, identifying and canceling common factors in rational expressions and applying the properties of positive integer exponents.*

What This Means

To answer questions assessed by the first learning standard (10.P.1), you must understand relations and functions. You may be asked to complete a pattern of numbers based on a rule. You may be given the rule or you may be asked to deduce it.

To answer questions assessed by the second learning standard (10.P.2), you must determine the slope or x- and y-intercepts of a line from either a graphical or algebraic representation. You must also understand the significance of a positive, negative, zero, or undefined slope.

Questions assessing the last two learning standards (10.P.3 and 10.P.4) require you to add, subtract, multiply, and divide polynomials.

STEP ONE TEN-MINUTE LESSON

Sample Problem 1

What is the missing number in the table for the function $3x + y = 9$?

x	y
1	6
2	3
3	?
4	−3

A. 0

B. −1

C. −2

D. −4

Ⓐ Ⓑ Ⓒ Ⓓ

Answer choice A: This is the correct answer. It results from properly substituting the given value for *x* and then solving for *y*.

Answer choice B: This answer is incorrect. It could result from either improper substitution or inaccurate solution of the resulting equation.

Answer choice C: This answer is incorrect. This answer might result if substitution was not properly accomplished.

Answer choice D: This answer is incorrect. This answer might result if substitution was correctly done but not properly solved for *y*.

Sample Problem 2

Look at the graph below.

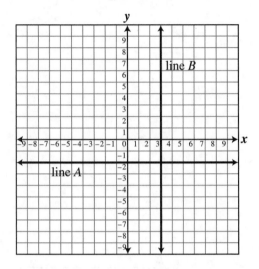

a. Calculate the slope of line *A*.

b. What is the significance of the slope of line *A*?

c. Calculate the slope of line *B*.

d. What is the significance of the slope of line *B*?

---

a. Answer: To answer this part of the question, choose any two points on line *A* and calculate the slope using the slope formula.

$$\text{slope} = \frac{y_2 - y_1}{x_2 - x_1}$$

Using points $(-3, -2)$ and $(2, -2)$, substitute the points into the formula.

$$\text{Slope} = \frac{-2 -(-2)}{2 -(-3)} = \frac{0}{5} = 0$$

b. Answer: Since the slope is 0, there is no change in the steepness of line *A*. Notice that line *A* is a horizontal line. Therefore, the slope of a horizontal line is 0.

c. Answer: Choose any two points on line *B* and find the slope. For example, if you use points $(3, 1)$ and $(3, -5)$, you will get

$$\frac{-5 - 1}{3 - 3} = \frac{-6}{0}$$

Division by 0 is not possible, so the slope of line *B* is undefined.

d. Answer: Notice that line *B* is a vertical line. Therefore, the slope of a vertical line is undefined.

STEP TWO | SIDEBAR INSTRUCTION

Complete the following problems. Use the Sidebar Instruction to help you choose the correct answer.

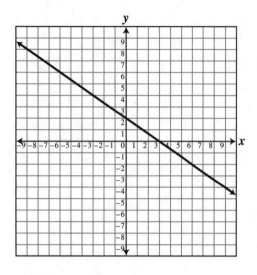

1 Which equation represents the line above?

A. $y = \frac{2}{3}x + 2$

B. $3y = 3x + 2$

C. $y = \frac{3}{2}x + 2$

D. $3y = -2x + 6$

Ⓐ Ⓑ Ⓒ Ⓓ

SIDEBAR INSTRUCTION

Remember that slope-intercept form for a line is

$y = mx + b$

where *m* is the slope of the line and *b* is the *y*-intercept.

Step 1: Write all equations in slope-intercept form.

$y = -\frac{2}{3}x + 2$

Step 2: Find the slope. You know that the slope is negative by the direction of the graph.

Step 3: Check your answer by checking the *y*-intercept and finding the *x*-intercept.

2 Simplify the expression below.

$$(\frac{y^2 + y}{y + 2}) \cdot (\frac{y^2 - 4}{y^2 + 3y})$$

A. $\dfrac{(y + 1)(y - 2)}{y + 3}$

B. $\dfrac{(y - 1)(y + 2)}{y + 3}$

C. $\dfrac{y^2 - y - 3}{y - 3}$

D. $\dfrac{y^2 + 1}{y + 3}$

Ⓐ Ⓑ Ⓒ Ⓓ

SIDEBAR INSTRUCTION

Factor each numerator and denominator. Then cancel a term if it appears in both the numerator and the denominator. Note that if a term appears in the numerator of one expression and the denominator of the other, it can still be cancelled since numerators are multiplied together and denominators are multiplied together.

3 Simplify the expression below.

$$\frac{(2x)^5}{2x^3}$$

A. x^8

B. $16x^2$

C. $4x^2$

D. x^2

Ⓐ Ⓑ Ⓒ Ⓓ

SIDEBAR INSTRUCTION

To solve this problem, first simplify the numerator. Then divide. Apply the Laws of Exponents. Let a and b represent any real numbers and m and n represent integers.

1. $a^m \cdot a^n = a^{m+n}$

2. $\dfrac{a^m}{a^n} = a^{m-n}$, if $a \neq 0$

3. $(ab)^m = a^m b^m$

4 Determine the x-intercept of the line $y = \dfrac{3}{5}x - 3$.

A. $(0, 0)$

B. $(-\dfrac{3}{5}, 0)$

C. $(\dfrac{5}{3}, 0)$

D. $(5, 0)$

Ⓐ Ⓑ Ⓒ Ⓓ

SIDEBAR INSTRUCTION

A graph intersects an axis when the value of the variable representing the other axis = 0. Set $y = 0$ and solve for x.

5 The graph of a linear equation intercepts the x-axis at $x = -4$ and passes through the point $(-6, 2)$. What is the equation of the line?

A. $y = -x - 4$

B. $y = \dfrac{1}{5}x - \dfrac{4}{5}$

C. $y = x + 4$

D. $y = -\dfrac{1}{5}x + \dfrac{4}{5}$

Ⓐ Ⓑ Ⓒ Ⓓ

SIDEBAR INSTRUCTION
You don't have to write the equation to solve this problem. Begin by using the process of elimination. Then choose the answer choice containing the correct equation.

6 The ordered pairs listed below represent points on a line. Find the slope of the line.

$$\{(2, -5), (-2, 7), (1, -2), (-1, 4)\}$$

A. 0

B. $-\dfrac{1}{5}$

C. -3

D. $\dfrac{1}{3}$

Ⓐ Ⓑ Ⓒ Ⓓ

SIDEBAR INSTRUCTION
Remember to use this formula to find the slope of a line:

$$\text{slope} = \dfrac{y_2 - y_1}{x_2 - x_1}$$

7 Determine the y-intercept of the equation $2y = -4x - 10$

A. $(0, -5)$

B. $(0, -10)$

C. $(0, 2.5)$

D. $(0, 10)$

Ⓐ Ⓑ Ⓒ Ⓓ

SIDEBAR INSTRUCTION
Remember that a graph intersects an axis when the value of the variable representing the other axis = 0.

8 A plumber charges $45 an hour plus $50 travel time to come to your house. The plumber's fee can be expressed with the function $f = 45(h) + 50$. Which is the independent quantity in this functional relationship?

A. the number of hours the plumber works

B. the distance to your house

C. the plumber's fee per hour

D. the fee for the travel time

Ⓐ   Ⓑ   Ⓒ   Ⓓ

SIDEBAR INSTRUCTION
The independent quantity is the amount within a function that can vary. It is the variable that affects the dependent quantity. Which answer choice can vary?

9 Keisha has received her first credit card, which has a $500 credit limit. She has charged a pair of shoes for $35, a jacket for $75, and a purse for $42. She has not yet made a payment on her credit card. Which inequality shows how much more, a, Keisha can purchase without going over her credit limit?

A. $a > \$152$

B. $a \leq \$152$

C. $a \leq \$348$

D. $a \geq \$348$

Ⓐ   Ⓑ   Ⓒ   Ⓓ

SIDEBAR INSTRUCTION
Subtract the total amount of Keisha's purchases from $500 to find how much more Keisha can purchase.

10 Which set of data could represent the same relationship as the graph?

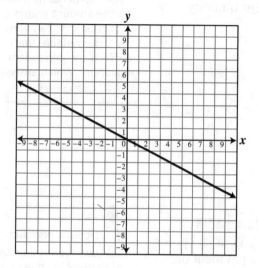

SIDEBAR INSTRUCTION

Attention needs to go to the tables after a brief examination of the graph. Notice that the line goes through the origin. Therefore, answer choice A is incorrect. Select ordered pairs from the other tables until two other choices are eliminated or a table is found in which all of the ordered pairs are on the line.

A.

x	y
−2	3
−1	2
0	1

C.

x	y
4	−2
2	−1
0	0

B.

x	y
−5	4
−2	2
0	0

D.

x	y
4	−2
3	−1
2	0

Ⓐ　Ⓑ　Ⓒ　Ⓓ

STEP THREE ON YOUR OWN

Complete the following problems. Choose the correct answer choice.

11 Which expression can be used to find the missing values of $f(x)$ in the table below?

x	$f(x)$
0	-2
1	0
2	6
3	16
4	?
5	?

A. $4x - 2$

B. $2x^2 - 2$

C. $2x^2 + 2$

D. $2x - 4$

Ⓐ   Ⓑ   Ⓒ   Ⓓ

12 Simplify the expression below.

$$\frac{x^2 + 1}{x^2 - 16} + \frac{5x + 3}{x^2 - 16}$$

A. $\dfrac{5x + 4}{x^2 - 32}$

B. $\dfrac{x + 1}{x - 4}$

C. $5x + \dfrac{3}{4}$

D. $\dfrac{x + 1}{x + 4}$

Ⓐ   Ⓑ   Ⓒ   Ⓓ

13 Analyze the table and find the missing number.

a	−2	−1	0	1	2	3
b	−7	−4	−1	2		8

A. 5

B. 3

C. 4

D. 7

Ⓐ   Ⓑ   Ⓒ   Ⓓ

14 What is the slope of the line below?

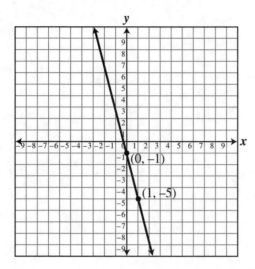

A. −4

B. $-\dfrac{1}{4}$

C. 2

D. 3

Ⓐ   Ⓑ   Ⓒ   Ⓓ

15 What are the coordinates of the *y*-intercept of the line $12y - 6x = 24$?

A. $(0, 2)$

B. $(-4, 0)$

C. $(2, 0)$

D. $(0, -4)$

Ⓐ   Ⓑ   Ⓒ   Ⓓ

16 What is the slope of the line below?

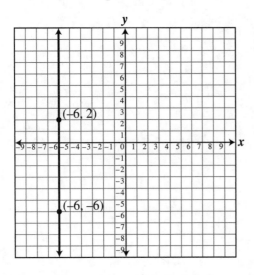

A. 1

B. −1

C. undefined

D. 0

Ⓐ   Ⓑ   Ⓒ   Ⓓ

...esent the graph of the line below?

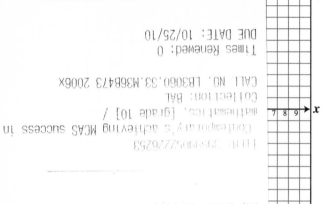

7 8 9 x

x	y
5	1
2	−1
−1	−3

x	y
−1	2
2	−1
−3	−1

18 Which number below is in the domain of the function below?

$$y = \frac{1}{\sqrt{x - 1}}$$

A. −1

B. 0

C. 2

D. 1

Ⓐ   Ⓑ   Ⓒ   Ⓓ

19 Which of the following is an equation of a line that passes through the points $(1, 8)$ and $(-2, -4)$?

A. $y = \frac{1}{4}x - 3.5$

B. $y = 2x + 2$

C. $y = \frac{1}{4}x - 2$

D. $y = 4x + 4$

Ⓐ   Ⓑ   Ⓒ   Ⓓ

20 If y varies directly as x, and $y = 12$ when $x = 8$, what is y when $x = 6$?

A. 9

B. 6

C. 12

D. 18

Ⓐ   Ⓑ   Ⓒ   Ⓓ

LESSON 6

PATTERNS, RELATIONS, AND ALGEBRA, PART 2

Learning Standards

10.P.5 *Find solutions to quadratic equations (with real roots) by factoring, completing the square, or using the quadratic formula. Demonstrate an understanding of the equivalence of the methods.*

10.P.6 *Solve equations and inequalities including those involving absolute value of linear expressions and apply to the solution of problems.*

10.P.7 *Solve everyday problems that can be modeled using linear, reciprocal, quadratic, or exponential functions. Apply appropriate tabular, graphical, or symbolic methods to the solution. Include compound interest, and direct and inverse variation problems. Use technology when appropriate.*

10.P.8 *Solve everyday problems that can be modeled using systems of linear equations or inequalities. Apply algebraic and graphical methods to the solution. Use technology when appropriate. Include mixture, rate, and work problems.*

What This Means

To answer questions assessing the first learning standard in this lesson (10.P.5), you need to know when it is most appropriate to use the methods of factoring, completing the square, and the quadratic formula to find solutions to quadratic equations. Sometimes you'll notice an expression that can be factored within an equation. When this happens, there will be two possible values for *x*. These values are often called the roots of the equation.

Learning standard 10.P.6 requires you to solve absolute value inequalities. For learning standards 10.P.7 and 10.P.8, you will apply all of the techniques that you have learned in solving linear and quadratic equations to real-world problems.

STEP ONE TEN-MINUTE LESSON

Sample Problem 1

Solve the inequality and graph its solution on a number line.

$$|2x - 4| < 2$$

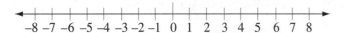

An absolute value inequality of the form

$|x + b| < a$

means that values of $(x + b)$ are between $-a$ and a:

$-a < (x + b) < a$

Rewrite the inequality in the above format and solve both inequalities at the same time.

$-2 < (2x - 4) < 2$

$-2 + 4 < 2x < 2 + 4$

$2 < 2x < 6$

$1 < x < 3$

The solution set includes all real numbers greater than 1 but less than 3.

The solution set is graphed below. Notice that there are open circles at 1 and 3. If the inequality had been written with a ≤ sign, the circles would be closed.

Sample Problem 2

What are the roots of the quadratic equation $x^2 + 4x - 21 = 0$?

A. $x = 21, x = 1$

B. $x = 7, x = -3$

C. $x = 14, x = 2$

D. $x = -7, x = 3$

Ⓐ   Ⓑ   Ⓒ   Ⓓ

Answer choice A: This answer is incorrect. It results from improper factoring. The factors that would result in these roots would not have produced a product of -21 or a sum of $+4$.

Answer choice B: This answer is incorrect. It results from improper factoring. The factors that would result in these roots would yield a product of -21 but not a sum of $+4$.

Answer choice C: The answer is incorrect. It results from improper factoring. The factors that would yield these roots could not be a product of any trinomial like the one given.

Answer choice D: This answer is correct. Obtaining two correct roots results from factoring properly, setting each factor equal to zero and solving the two resulting equations.

STEP TWO SIDEBAR INSTRUCTION

Complete the following problems. Use the Sidebar Instruction to help you choose the correct answer.

1 The perimeter of a given equilateral triangle varies directly as the length of a side. If the perimeter of an altered equilateral triangle is now 25% of what it was, what happens to the length of each side?

_____

_____

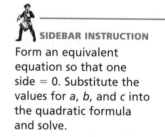

SIDEBAR INSTRUCTION
Determine the ratio of the perimeters of the given triangle and the altered triangle. Use that ratio to decribe the length of the side of the altered triangle compared to the given triangle.

2 Solve for both roots of the equation $2x^2 - 12 = -5x$.

A. $x = 2\frac{1}{2}$, $x = 5$

B. $x = -1\frac{1}{2}$, $x = 4$

C. $x = 1\frac{1}{2}$, $x = -4$

D. $x = -2\frac{1}{2}$, $x = -5$

SIDEBAR INSTRUCTION
Form an equivalent equation so that one side = 0. Substitute the values for *a*, *b*, and *c* into the quadratic formula and solve.

3 The cost per person at a wedding varies inversely as the number of guests. If 100 people attend the wedding, the cost is $125 per person. How many guests are attending the wedding if the cost per person is $50?

A. 125

B. 250

C. 200

D. 150

Ⓐ Ⓑ Ⓒ Ⓓ

SIDEBAR INSTRUCTION

If *y* varies inversely as *x*, then

$$xy = k$$

where *k* is the constant of variation.

Let *y* equal the cost per person, and *x* equal the number of people attending. Find *k* by substituting the initial values into the equation. Next, substitute the value of *k* and the new value for *y* into the equation and solve for *x*, the number of people attending.

4 As part of Peter's job at a construction company, he has to haul 2 tons of sand in the company's truck, which can carry *x* pounds at a time. In terms of *x*, how many trips will Peter have to make?

A. $\dfrac{2}{x}$ trips

B. $4{,}000x$ trips

C. $\dfrac{4{,}000}{x}$ trips

D. $2{,}000x$ trips

Ⓐ Ⓑ Ⓒ Ⓓ

SIDEBAR INSTRUCTION

First, change 2 tons to the equivalent number of pounds. Then choose the mathematical operation you need to calculate the number of trips.

5 Susan and her brother Rick together have $48. Susan has three times as much money as Rick. How much money does Susan have?

A. $48

B. $36

C. $24

D. $16

Ⓐ Ⓑ Ⓒ Ⓓ

SIDEBAR INSTRUCTION

Let *m* represent the amount of money Rick has. Let *3m* represent the amount of money Susan has. Together, they have $48. Write this statement in terms of *m*:

$$m + 3m = \$48.$$

Solve for *m*.

Question 6 is a short-answer question. Write your answer on the lines below.

6 Find the roots of the quadratic equation below.

$x^2 - 10x + 9 = 0$

SIDEBAR INSTRUCTION

Attempts at factoring the trinomial should prove successful. After setting each factor = 0, solve and find the roots.

_____

_____

7 Which pair of points are roots of the function graphed below?

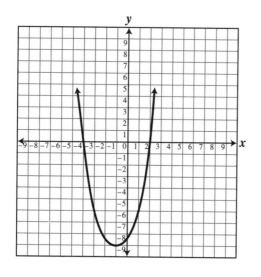

SIDEBAR INSTRUCTION

If a quadratic function is graphed, the roots of the function are the two points where the graph intersects the x-axis. An ordered pair is a root of the equation only if it lies on the graph of that equation. The correct answer is the choice where both ordered pairs lie on the graph.

A. $(-1, -9), (0, -8)$

B. $(0, -4), (2, 0)$

C. $(-4, 0), (2, 0)$

D. $(0, 2), (0, -4)$

(A)   (B)   (C)   (D)

8 Which statement best represents the following relationship between spending per student and average teacher salary?

SIDEBAR INSTRUCTION
To find the percent one number is of another, divide. Then multiply the quotient by 100.

State	Spending per Student	Average Teacher Salary
New Jersey	$9,500	$45,000
Connecticut	$8,000	$49,500
New York	$7,500	$47,000
Pennsylvania	$7,000	$43,500
Alaska	$8,500	$46,500

A. No relationship can be determined from the data in the table.

B. The greater the spending per student, the higher the teacher's salary.

C. When compared as a percent of teacher's salary, New Jersey spends the most per pupil.

D. The ratio of spending per pupil to the average teacher salary is the same in all states.

Ⓐ Ⓑ Ⓒ Ⓓ

9 A mail-order company that sells T-shirts charges $1.50 to ship the first T-shirt, then an additional $0.25 cents for each shirt thereafter. If the function $y = 0.25(x - 1) + 1.50$ expresses an order's total shipping cost, what does the variable x represent?

A. The cost of shipping one shirt

B. One less than the total number of shirts

C. The total cost of the order including shipping

D. The total number of shirts in the order

Ⓐ Ⓑ Ⓒ Ⓓ

SIDEBAR INSTRUCTION
Think about what the problem tells us. The correct answer will be a variable that would be diminished by 1 and multiplied by 0.25(25¢).

STEP THREE ON YOUR OWN

Complete the following problems. Choose the correct answer choice.

10 Kiera and her family average 54 mph on the highway. If they go on a $6\frac{1}{2}$ hour trip, how far do they travel?

A. 257 miles

B. 351 miles

C. 540 miles

D. 724 miles

Ⓐ   Ⓑ   Ⓒ   Ⓓ

11 Eric has a rectangular garden. The width of the garden is 3 yards less than the length. If the area is 18 square yards, how many yards of fencing will Eric need to enclose the garden?

A. 9 yd

B. 12 yd

C. 15 yd

D. 18 yd

Ⓐ   Ⓑ   Ⓒ   Ⓓ

Question 12 is a short-answer question. Write your answer on the lines below.

12 Together, Tyler, Morgan, and Sam worked 210 hours volunteering at their local community center during the year. Morgan worked 10 more hours than Sam, and Tyler worked twice as many hours as Morgan. How many hours did Morgan work at the community center during the year.

Show your work.

_____

_____

_____

_____

13 What are the roots of the quadratic equation $2x^2 - 16x + 10 = 0$?

A. $x = 4 + \sqrt{11}, x = 4 - \sqrt{11}$

B. $x = 2, x = -2$

C. $x = 4 + 2\sqrt{3}, x = 4 - 2\sqrt{3}$

D. $x = 8, x = -8$

Ⓐ Ⓑ Ⓒ Ⓓ

14 Which of the following equations represent a quadratic function?

A. $y^2 = x$

B. $y^2 + x^2 = 9$

C. $7x + 3 = y$

D. $-2x^2 + y = 3 + x$

Ⓐ Ⓑ Ⓒ Ⓓ

15 Which variable is the independent variable in the following equation?

$$y = \frac{x^2 - 1}{x + 1}$$

A. either x or y

B. y only

C. both x and y

D. x only

Ⓐ Ⓑ Ⓒ Ⓓ

16 Enrique has 14 more nickels than dimes. If the total value of these coins is $6.10, what is the number of nickels that Enrique has?

A. 50

B. 49

C. 40

D. 36

Ⓐ Ⓑ Ⓒ Ⓓ

LESSON 7

Learning Standards

10.D.1 *Select, create, and interpret an appropriate graphical representation (e.g., scatterplot, table, stem-and-leaf plots, box-and-whisker plots, circle graph, line graph, and line plot) for a set of data and use appropriate statistics (e.g., mean, median, range, and mode) to communicate information about the data. Use these notions to compare different sets of data.*

10.D.2 *Approximate a line of best fit (trend line) given a set of data (e.g. scatterplot). Use technology when appropriate.*

10.D.3 *Describe and explain how the relative sizes of a sample and the population affect the validity of predictions from a set of data.*

What This Means

Questions assessed by these learning standards require you to interpret information in different ways. You may be given information about a sample of something and asked to draw a conclusion about the entire amount. You need to set up a proportion to solve these problems.

Some questions assessed by these learning standards will require you to make an observation about a population based on data collected by only some individuals. The mean, median, and mode are three measures of central tendency for a data set. You might encounter one or two of these questions on the MCAS.

You will most likely be asked to interpret information from different types of graphs and tables. While these types of question are not the most difficult on the test, they can sometimes be tricky. Make sure that you are interpreting the information correctly.

STEP ONE **TEN-MINUTE LESSON**

Sample Problem 1

Cole is conducting research for a school report in which he investigated how many households in his neighborhood have received the morning newspaper in the past 4 years. He made the bar graph below.

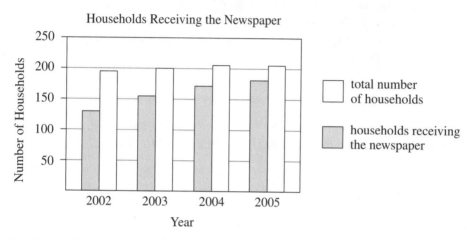

During which year was the percentage of households receiving the morning newspaper the highest?

A. 2002

B. 2003

C. 2004

D. 2005

Ⓐ Ⓑ Ⓒ Ⓓ

To solve this problem, you need to calculate the percentage for each year. To do this, divide the total number of households into the number of households receiving the newspaper. You can also see this information displayed in the bar graph. The year with the higher percentage is the year where the number of households receiving the newspaper is closet to the total number of households.

Answer choice A: The percentage for this answer choice is about 71%. This is probably not the highest percentage.

Answer choice B: The percentage for this answer choice is 80%. This is higher than answer choice A, but you need to consider each answer choice before making a decision.

Answer choice C: This percentage is 83%. This is higher than answer choices A and B, but it may not be the highest.

Answer choice D: This percentage is about 86%, the highest of all years polled. This is the correct answer choice.

Sample Problem 2

Sam and his friends are playing a game in which they spin an arrow on a circle divided into four sections: yellow, red, green, and yellow. Each time the arrow spins, it stops on one of the sections of the circle. It is Sam's turn to spin the arrow. Assume that the arrow never stops on a line. What is the probability that the arrow will land on yellow?

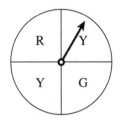

A. $\frac{1}{4}$

B. $\frac{1}{2}$

C. $\frac{1}{3}$

D. $\frac{2}{3}$

Ⓐ   Ⓑ   Ⓒ   Ⓓ

To solve this problem, you need to determine what percent of the spinner is yellow. The probability is $\frac{2}{4} = \frac{1}{2}$. The spinner has four sections and two of these sections are yellow.

Answer choice A: This answer indicates that out of a total of 4 sections on which the spinner can stop, there is only one section that would provide success. This is not the correct answer.

Answer choice B: The probability of the spinner landing on a yellow section is 2 out of 4 total sections or $\frac{2}{4} = \frac{1}{2}$. This is the correct answer.

Answer choice C: There are not 3 total sections and there is more than one yellow section. This is not the correct answer.

Answer choice D: There are not 3 ways in total, but there are two yellow sections. This is not the correct answer.

STEP TWO SIDEBAR INSTRUCTION

Complete the following problems. Use the Sidebar Instruction to help you choose the best answer.

1 This is a stem-and-leaf plot of test scores received by students on their American History midterm. Using the information from this stem-and-leaf plot, find the mean score. (Round to the nearest tenth.)

9 | 3 2 0 0

8 | 9 7 3 3 1

7 | 8 7

6 | 9 4 4

5 | 2 0

A. 83

B. 81

C. 77.6

D. 64

Ⓐ   Ⓑ   Ⓒ   Ⓓ

SIDEBAR INSTRUCTION

The stem-and-leaf plot is a way to organize numbers so that you can analyze them. The first number (before the straight line) indicates the "tens." 9|3 is 93, 9|2 is 92. In this stem-and-leaf plot, there are four scores in the 90s, five scores in the 80s, two scores in the 70s, and so on. As a reminder, the mean is the average of the scores.

2 Carly had accumulated the following scores on her math tests: 81, 81, 82, 80, 79, 81, 80, 81, 82, 80. What was the mode of her scores?

A. 82

B. 81

C. 80

D. 79

Ⓐ   Ⓑ   Ⓒ   Ⓓ

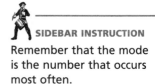

SIDEBAR INSTRUCTION

Remember that the mode is the number that occurs most often.

3 This diagram of a tabletop is made of gray and white tiles. Nick throws a coin. What is the probability that the coin will land on a gray tile?

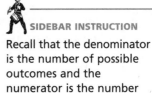

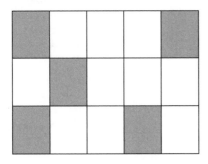

A. $\frac{1}{2}$

B. $\frac{1}{3}$

C. $\frac{1}{4}$

D. $\frac{1}{5}$

Ⓐ   Ⓑ   Ⓒ   Ⓓ

4 The box-and-whisker plot shows a set of numbers. Which number is the greatest number in the data set?

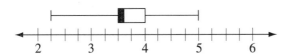

A. 3.0

B. 4.0

C. 4.5

D. 5.0

Ⓐ   Ⓑ   Ⓒ   Ⓓ

5 A box contains 4 nickels, 3 dimes, 4 quarters, and 1 penny. What is the probability of picking a nickel from the box?

A. $\dfrac{1}{2}$

B. $\dfrac{1}{3}$

C. $\dfrac{1}{4}$

D. $\dfrac{1}{12}$

Ⓐ   Ⓑ   Ⓒ   Ⓓ

SIDEBAR INSTRUCTION

Recall that probability is the number of favorable outcomes divided by the total number of possible outcomes.

6 Manuel has test scores of 70, 80, 100, 88, and 84. What does he have to get on his next test to get an 85 average?

A. 80

B. 85

C. 86

D. 88

Ⓐ   Ⓑ   Ⓒ   Ⓓ

SIDEBAR INSTRUCTION

Find the mean of Manuel's test scores. Then determine which answer choice would bring his average up to 85.

STEP THREE ON YOUR OWN

Complete each of the following problems. Choose the correct answer choice.

Question 7 is a short-answer question. Write your answer on the lines below.

7 The high temperatures in seven Arizona cities were recorded one day. They were 96°F, 99°F, 102°F, 101°F, 99°F, 106°F, 97°F, 100°F. What was the median high temperatures among these cities on that day?

_____

_____

_____

8 Sumita has a pair of number cubes. Each cube has 6 faces with each face representing a different number from 1 to 6. She rolls the number cubes. What is the probability that the sum of the numbers rolled is 7?

A. $\frac{1}{3}$

B. $\frac{1}{6}$

C. $\frac{1}{12}$

D. $\frac{1}{36}$

Ⓐ Ⓑ Ⓒ Ⓓ

9 Luba bought 2 cans of white paint, 2 cans of beige paint, and 4 cans of green paint. When she returned home, she realized that the cans had not been labeled. What is the probability that the first can she opens will be beige?

A. $\frac{1}{4}$

B. $\frac{1}{2}$

C. $\frac{1}{3}$

D. $\frac{2}{3}$

Ⓐ Ⓑ Ⓒ Ⓓ

10 The height in inches of five of Rachel's friends is listed below.

66, 61, 61, 67, 68

Which of these measures of central tendency would yield the **greatest** value?

A. mean

B. median

C. mode

D. range

Ⓐ Ⓑ Ⓒ Ⓓ

11 What is the likelihood of flipping a coin 3 times with it turning up heads all three times?

A. $\frac{1}{2}$

B. $\frac{1}{4}$

C. $\frac{1}{6}$

D. $\frac{1}{8}$

Ⓐ Ⓑ Ⓒ Ⓓ

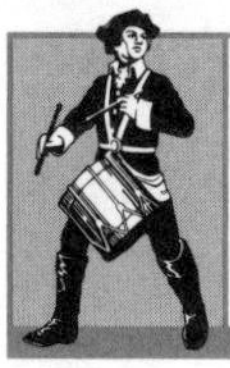

REVIEW 3

This section reviews the learning standards for Lessons 5, 6, and 7. Choose the correct answer choice.

1 What is the slope of a line that passes through the points (2, 4) and (−7, −10)?

A. $-\dfrac{14}{9}$

B. $\dfrac{3}{2}$

C. $\dfrac{14}{9}$

D. $-\dfrac{3}{2}$

Ⓐ Ⓑ Ⓒ Ⓓ

2 What are the roots of the equation below?

$$2x^2 + 28x - 102 = 0$$

A. $x = 21, x = 3$

B. $x = 17, x = -3$

C. $x = 34, x = -6$

D. $x = 3, x = -17$

Ⓐ Ⓑ Ⓒ Ⓓ

3 Solve the inequality and graph its solution set below.

$|3x - 6| \leq 3$

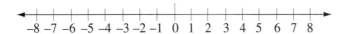

4 There are 3 less than twice as many men as there are women in Bailey's English class. There are 30 students in the class. How many students are women?

A. 21

B. 19

C. 11

D. 9

Ⓐ Ⓑ Ⓒ Ⓓ

5 Multiply. Express in simplest form.

$$\left(\frac{4x^2 - 16x}{2x^2 - 32}\right) \cdot \left(\frac{(x + 4)^2}{8x^2}\right)$$

A. $\dfrac{x + 4}{x}$

B. $\dfrac{2x\,(x + 2)}{x + 4}$

C. $\dfrac{x + 4}{4x}$

D. $\dfrac{x + 4}{2x\,(x + 2)}$

Ⓐ   Ⓑ   Ⓒ   Ⓓ

6 Two number cubes labeled 1 through 6 are tossed. What is the probability that the sum of the two numbers rolled is a number divisible by 3?

A. $\dfrac{4}{9}$

B. $\dfrac{5}{18}$

C. $\dfrac{1}{3}$

D. $\dfrac{1}{2}$

Ⓐ   Ⓑ   Ⓒ   Ⓓ

7 The stem and leaf plot below indicates the weights of the front line players on the Elmwood Pop Warner Football team. What is the mean weight to the nearest pound?

6 | 1 3 8

7 | 4 6

8 | 2 8

A. 73 lb

B. 74 lb

C. 75 lb

D. 78 lb

Ⓐ Ⓑ Ⓒ Ⓓ

Posttest

MASSACHUSETTS COMPREHENSIVE ASSESSMENT SYSTEM
Grade 10 Mathematics Reference Sheet

AREA FORMULAS

triangle .... $A = \frac{1}{2}bh$

rectangle ...... $A = bh$

square .... $A = s^2$

trapezoid ..... $A = \frac{1}{2}h(b_1 + b_2)$

CIRCLE FORMULAS

$C = 2\pi r$

$A = \pi r^2$

VOLUME FORMULAS

cube .... $V = s^3$
(s = length of an edge)

rectangular prism .... $V = lwh$
OR
$V = Bh$

(B = area of the base)

sphere .... $V = \frac{4}{3}\pi r^3$

right circular cylinder .... $V = \pi r^2 h$

right circular cone .... $V = \frac{1}{3}\pi r^2 h$

right square pyramid .... $V = \frac{1}{3}s^2 h$

LATERAL SURFACE AREA FORMULAS

rectangular prism .... $LA = 2(hw) + 2(lh)$

right circular cylinder .... $LA = 2\pi rh$

right circular cone .... $LA = \pi r\ell$

right square pyramid .... $LA = 2s\ell$

(ℓ = slant height)

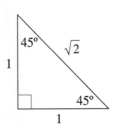

TOTAL SURFACE AREA FORMULAS

cube .... $SA = 6s^2$

rectangular prism .... $SA = 2(lw) + 2(hw) + 2(lh)$

sphere .... $SA = 4\pi r^2$

right circular cylinder .... $SA = 2\pi r^2 + 2\pi rh$

right circular cone .... $SA = \pi r^2 + \pi r\ell$

right square pyramid .... $SA = s^2 + 2s\ell$

(ℓ = slant height)

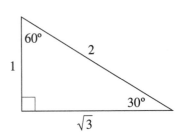

130

SESSION 1

You may use your reference sheet during this session.
*You may **not** use a calculator during this session.*

DIRECTIONS

This session contains fourteen multiple-choice questions, four short-answer questions, and three open-response questions. Mark your answers to these questions in the spaces provided in your Posttest Answer Booklet (page 161).

1 If $-27 \leq x^3 < 8$, which of the following shows the range of possible values of x?

A.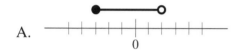

B.

C.

D.

2 To find the roots of the equation $x^2 - 2x = -6$, which of the following values of a, b, and c should be used in the quadratic formula?

A. $a = 1, b = 2, c = 6$

B. $a = -1, b = 2, c = -6$

C. $a = -1, b = -2, c = 6$

D. $a = 1, b = -2, c = 6$

Go On

3 If the radius of a sphere is doubled, what will be the effect on its surface area?

A. The surface area will be increased by a factor of 2.

B. The surface area will be increased by a factor of 3.

C. The surface area will be increased by a factor of 4.

D. The surface area will be increased by a factor of 16.

4 Which of the lines below is perpendicular to the line $\frac{1}{3}x - y = -2$

A. $y = \frac{1}{3}x + 2$

B. $y = 4 - 3x$

C. $y = 1$

D. $y = 3$

5 Which of the following functions has the greatest value for $x = 5$?

A. $f(x) = x^3 + 3x$

B. $f(x) = 20x + 5$

C. $f(x) = 1^x$

D. $f(x) = x^4 - x^3 - x^2$

6 Which equation describes the line of the graph below?

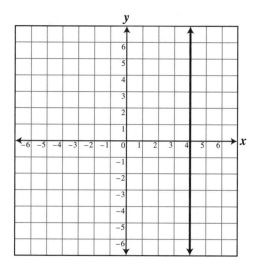

A. $x = 4$

B. $y = x$

C. $y = 2x - 24$

D. $x = y$

7 Which of the following statements is always true?

A. The product of two odd numbers is even.

B. The square root of a rational number is irrational.

C. The quotient of two rational numbers is rational.

D. The sum of two rational numbers is greater than either of the numbers.

Go On

8 Which equation below describes a line that passes through the point (3, 7) and is perpendicular to the line $-\dfrac{1}{3}x + y = 6$.

A. $y = -3x + 16$

B. $y = 3x + 8$

C. $y = \dfrac{1}{3}x + 16$

D. $y = -\dfrac{1}{3}x + 8$

9 The area of $\square ABCD$ is 100. What is the area of the inscribed circle shown in the diagram below?

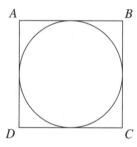

A. 100π

B. 50π

C. 25π

D. 10π

10 What is the value of $\dfrac{\sqrt{4x^4}}{4x^2}$

    A. 1

    B. x

    C. $\dfrac{1}{2}$

    D. 4

11 If the measure of minor arc $\overset{\frown}{AB}$ is 80°, what is the value of x?

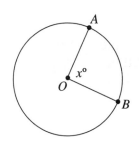

    A. 20°

    B. 62°

    C. 80°

    D. 72°

Go On

12 Which of the following is equivalent to $\dfrac{\sqrt{128}}{\sqrt{20}}$?

    A. $8\sqrt{2}$

    B. $\dfrac{4\sqrt{2}}{\sqrt{5}}$

    C. $\dfrac{2\sqrt{32}}{\sqrt{10}}$

    D. $\dfrac{4\sqrt{1}}{\sqrt{5}}$

13 A manufacturer produces metal railroad track in 4-meter lengths. A piece of track can differ from the perfect 4-meter length by 0.0001 meter and still be acceptable. Which of the following equations could be used to represent this situation?

    A. $|x - 4| \le 0.0001$

    B. $|x + 4| \le 0.0001$

    C. $|4 + 0.0001| \le x$

    D. $|x - 0.0001| \le 4$

14 If $f(x) = \dfrac{x^2 - x}{4}$, find $f(-4)$.

    A. $\sqrt{3}$

    B. 3

    C. 5

    D. $\sqrt{5}$

Questions 15 and 16 are short-answer questions. Write your answers to these questions in the boxes provided in your Posttest Answer Booklet.

15 The floor of a bank vault will be made of poured concrete. The floor will be 2 feet thick, 10 feet wide, and 15 feet long. If concrete can be poured at a rate of 5 cubic feet per minute, how long will it take to create the floor?

16 The mean of 46, 60, 54, 52, x, and y is 53. y is 10 more than x. Solve for x and y.

Question 17 is an open-response question.

17   **Given:** $\angle AOB \cong \angle COD$

      Prove: $\triangle AOB \cong \triangle COD$ **without** using the Side-Angle-Side Postulate.

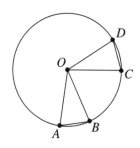

Statement	Reason
1. $\angle AOB \cong COD$	1. Given
2. $\overline{AO} \cong \overline{CO}$	2.
3. $\overline{AB} \cong \overline{CD}$	3.
4. $\dfrac{AO}{BO} \cong \dfrac{CO}{DO}$	4.
5. $\triangle AOB \cong \triangle COD$	5.

Questions 18 and 19 are short-answer questions. Write your answers to these questions in the boxes provided in your Posttest Answer Booklet.

18 The cost per person to hold a wedding reception at a catering hall varies inversely as the number of people attending the reception. If 100 people attend, the cost is $120 each. How many people are attending the reception if the cost per person is $80?

19 Simplify the expression:

$$3^4 - 3(6^2 - 4^3) - (3^2 - 2)^0$$

Go On ▶

Questions 20 and 21 are open-response questions.

- **BE SURE TO ANSWER AND LABEL ALL PARTS OF EACH QUESTION.**
- **Show all your work (diagrams, tables, or computations) in your Posttest Answer Booklet.**
- **If you do the work in your head, explain in writing how you did the work.**

Write your answer to question 20 in the space provided in your Posttest Answer Booklet.

 A square and a triangle have the same area. The length of the base of the triangle is 10 inches more than four times the length of a side of the square. The height of the triangle is 6 inches less than the length of a side of the square.

   a. Sketch and label a diagram that fits the situation.

   b. Find the length of the side of the square.

   c. In solving for the length of the side of the square, is there more than one possible solution? Why or why not?

Write your answer to question 21 in the space provided in your Posttest Answer Booklet.

21 Two video rental stores offer two different rental prices. Store A charges $3.00 for each video that is rented. Store B charges $10.00 for membership and $1.00 for each video that is rented.

    a. Write an equation that shows the total cost, *c*, of renting *n* videos from store A.

    b. Write an equation that shows the total cost, *c*, of renting *n* videos from store B.

    c. Graph and label the equation from part *a* and part *b* on the same set of axes. Use the graph on the Posttest Answer Booklet.

    d. According to the graphs drawn in part *c*, for what number of video rentals is the cost of membership in the two clubs the same?

SESSION 2

You may use your reference sheet during this session.
*You may **not** use a calculator during this session.*

DIRECTIONS:

This session contains eighteen multiple-choice questions and three open-response questions. Mark your answers to these questions in the spaces provided in your Posttest Answer Booklet.

 Using the method which can always be used to find the roots of a quadratic equation, find the roots for this equation, $2x^2 = 9$.

A. $\pm 9\sqrt{2}$

B. $\dfrac{\pm 5\sqrt{2}}{2}$

C. $\dfrac{\pm 3\sqrt{2}}{2}$

D. $\pm 3\sqrt{2}$

23 The table below shows the average monthly sales of automobiles by brand at an automobile dealership.

Brand	Average Monthly Sales
Acura	15
Infiniti	10
Lexus	25
BMW	30
Mercedes	45

What is the probability that the next car sold will be a Mercedes or a BMW?

A. $\dfrac{45}{125}$

B. $\dfrac{30}{125}$

C. $\dfrac{45 \times 30}{125}$

D. $\dfrac{75}{125}$

24 What is the next number in the sequence below?

1, 2, 3, 5, 8, 13

A. 19

B. 18

C. 21

D. 17

Go On

25 George and Gracey are planning to build a pool in back of their house as shown in the diagram below. The distance from the back of the house to the end of the property is 67 feet. However, due to the composition of the soil, they will now have to build the pool so that it is rotated 90 degrees in a clockwise direction from their original plan. How far from the end of the property will the pool be?

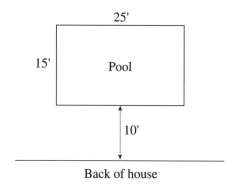

A. 38 feet

B. 28 feet

C. 48 feet

D. 32 feet

26 In the isosceles triangle below, $\angle A \cong \angle C$. The length of AB is 14 less than twice the length of AC. The perimeter of the triangle is 32 units. What is the area of the triangle?

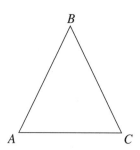

A. 12 square units

B. 24 square units

C. 36 square units

D. 48 square units

144

27 Which equation describes the line of symmetry of the figure below?

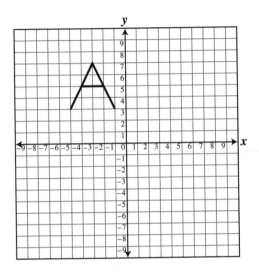

A. $y = 3$

B. $x = -3$

C. $y = -3$

D. $x = 3$

28 The table below represents the monthly rent that each of five friends pays for their separate apartments.

Friend	Rent
John	$1,100
Amy	$2,000
Susan	$1,800
Darrell	
Maurice	$1,700

The mean rent for the five friends is $1,600. How much rent does Darrell pay?

A. $1,400

B. $1,500

C. $1,600

D. $1,700

29 What type of function is described by the values in the following table?

x	$f(x)$
0	0
1	2
2	5
−1	2
−2	5

A. Linear

B. Step

C. Quadratic

D. Exponential

30 A standard sugar cone used as an ice-cream cone has a height of approximately 5 inches and a radius of 1 inch. If you wanted to triple the amount of ice cream that the cone itself holds by increasing the radius of the cone, what is the best estimation of the new radius?

A. 1.4 inches

B. 1.7 inches

C. 1.9 inches

D. 2.0 inches

Question 31 is an open-response question.

- **BE SURE TO ANSWER AND LABEL ALL PARTS OF EACH QUESTION.**
- **Show all your work (diagrams, tables, or computations) in your Posttest Answer Booklet.**
- **If you do the work in your head, explain in writing how you did the work.**

Write your answer to question 31 in the space provided in your Posttest Answer Booklet.

31 In the quadratic formula $x = \dfrac{-b \pm \sqrt{b^2 - 4ac}}{2a}$, the expression $b^2 - 4ac$ is sometimes called the *discriminant*. Write and simplify the discriminant for the equation $3x^2 + 4x = 8$.

Go On

Mark your answers to multiple-choice questions 32 through 40 in the spaces provided in your Posttest Answer Booklet.

32 An ice cube tray is 10 inches long, 2 inches deep and 1 inch high. Each block of ice is a perfect cube with sides measuring 1 inch. What is the surface area of one of the cubes?

A. 6 square inches

B. 8 square inches

C. 10 square inches

D. 12 square inches

33 Which of the following pairs of points identifies a line with slope $-\dfrac{3}{5}$?

A. (1, 4) and (3, 7)

B. (−5, 4) and (0, 7)

C. (−3, 1) and (7, −5)

D. (−1, 5) and (1, 2)

34 On a certain map 2.5 inches represents 100 miles. If two cities are 1.5 feet apart on the map, what is the distance between them in miles?

A. 0.45 miles

B. 720 miles

C. 1,440 miles

D. 0.65 miles

35 A diagonal of square *ABCD* measures $11\sqrt{2}$. What is the area of the square?

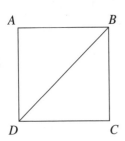

A. 242

B. $22\sqrt{2}$

C. 44

D. 121

36 The exterior wall of a cylindrical grain silo needs to be painted. If the radius of the silo is 10.3 feet and the height is 20.7 feet, what is the approximate surface area of the exterior wall?

A. 213π

B. 426π

C. 532π

D. 638π

37 Two number cubes are rolled. What is the probability that the sum of the two numbers rolled is a number evenly divisible by 3?

A. $\dfrac{2}{9}$

B. $\dfrac{1}{4}$

C. $\dfrac{5}{18}$

D. $\dfrac{1}{3}$

Go On

38 Every 40 minutes, the hour hand on a clock moves through an angle of how many degrees?

A. 10°

B. 20°

C. 40°

D. 240°

39 The mean weight of the offensive line at Curry High School is 320 pounds. Which statement is true?

A. All players weigh 320 pounds.

B. The heaviest player is 320 pounds.

C. The average weight of the players is 320 pounds.

D. Most of the players weigh less than 320 pounds.

40 Perform the indicated operation.

$$\frac{4z^2 - 24z - 28}{2z - 14} \cdot \frac{1}{z + 1}$$

A. 2

B. $2z - 14$

C. 1

D. $2z + 2$

Question 41 is an open-response question.

- **BE SURE TO ANSWER AND LABEL ALL PARTS OF EACH QUESTION.**
- **Show all your work (diagrams, tables, or computations) in your Posttest Answer Booklet.**
- **If you do the work in your head, explain in writing how you did the work.**

Write your answer to question 41 in the space provided in your Posttest Answer Booklet.

 The chart below shows the test scores and the number of students who received that same score on a recent test in Mr. Lee's math class.

Number of Students	Test Scores
3	95
9	85
5	75
2	68
1	50

a. What is the mean grade? Round your answer to the nearest tenth.

b. What is the median grade?

c. What is the mode?

Go On

Question 42 is an open-response question.

- **BE SURE TO ANSWER AND LABEL ALL PARTS OF EACH QUESTION.**
- Show all your work (diagrams, tables, or computations) in your Posttest Answer Booklet.
- If you do the work in your head, explain in writing how you did the work.

Write your answer to question 42 in the space provided in your Posttest Answer Booklet.

42 The table below shows the number of homes sold by a realty company during the first 6 months of 2004.

Month	Number of Homes Sold
January	16
February	12
March	14
April	7
May	10
June	3

a. On the grid in the Posttest Answer Booklet, plot the data using the months of the year on the *x*-axis and the number of homes sold on the *y*-axis.

b. Draw a single straight line that best represents the data.

c. Explain why you drew your line as you did.

BE SURE YOU HAVE RECORDED ALL OF YOUR ANSWERS IN YOUR POSTTEST ANSWER BOOKLET.

GREYSCALE

BIN TRAVELER FORM

Cut By: DaVonhee   Qty 34   Date 11-14-24

Scanned By: _____   Qty _____   Date _____

Scanned Batch IDs

Notes / Exception